Caring for Mom and Other Loved Souls

A Journey of Love and Loss

Diane Doran Blum

Dedication

In memory of my parents, Ed and Dee.

They taught me everything about the importance of family, kindness, and love.

I hope they're enjoying heaven
as much as I'm sure the angels appreciate having them there.

Foreword

By Dr. Anna Cabeca

In addition to being a mom, doctor (triple-board-certified and a fellow of gynecology and obstetrics, integrative medicine, and anti-aging and regenerative medicine), and best-selling author of *The Hormone Fix*, I was a caregiver to both my parents. My caregiving journey started when my mother was diagnosed with diabetes and heart disease. She was in and out of hospitals for fifteen years, passing away at the young age of sixty-seven.

My dad did well for many years after my mother's death, but as he aged, his health started to decline. By the age of seventy-nine, I saw a dramatic change in his vibrancy, and some days he could barely walk. One day I asked him if I could talk with his doctors, and with his permission I did. They seemed to feel, "He's seventy-nine after all… and he's had a good run," so not to worry!

But I knew my dad had many good years left, he only needed my holistic medical expertise to healthfully age. I started him on a detox and nutrition program and fine-tuned his hormones. His health dramatically improved, and he lived happily and healthily until the age of ninety-one.

During that decade-plus of caregiving, my family was blessed to have my dad frequently in our lives. I will always be appreciative that my four daughters got the opportunity to spend so much time with him, to love and learn from him.

Studies have shown that multigenerational households are a marker of longevity for both young and old family members.[1] People living in larger households are at reduced risk of dying from dementia due to the increased connection and engagement they have with their family. This stimulates oxytocin (our hormone of bonding and happiness), having anti-stress effects on our well-being.[2]

True, caregiving is a double-edged sword. It can be intense, exhausting, and stressful. But when I look back on those years, no matter how difficult, I simply breathe and give thanks for all the time and all the blessings I had with my parents. As caregivers, we must cherish those times.

In this book, the author tells a beautiful story of her own caregiving experiences, which she calls the "blessings and stressings" of caregiving. I love how she details the mental and emotional challenges of caring for a loved one, providing practical advice and inspiration from her own and other carers' most intimate stories.

I think you will enjoy Diane and her family's journey. Remember to stay present in the moment, find joy with the one you are caring for, and don't sweat the small stuff. You are only human and doing your best.

Anna Cabeca, DO, OBGYN, FACOG

Table of Contents

Chapter 1

What does a caregiving journey look like?

Most of you will spend time as a caregiver at some point during your life. Perhaps you are already in the midst of that journey.

For those of you who are lucky, you will get to watch your parents grow old. At some point, you or a sibling may find yourself helping with—or in charge of—their ongoing or end-of-life care. At the same time, you may also be raising your own family, perhaps with very young children. You may still be working. Or, you may need to care for an elderly or disabled spouse, possibly dealing with dementia or other disabilities.

Although rewarding, each of these caregiving scenarios will likely involve challenges with family members, the care receiver's doctors, and even with the loved one themselves. While many of these stressors will be centered on the daily, physical requirements of caregiving, the mental and emotional effects over the long haul will often be more difficult for most caregivers to successfully navigate. They certainly were for me, and thus became the inspiration for this book.

I spent decades as a caregiver, raising two sons while focusing on my parents' care. But now, my sons are young adults, and both my parents are gone.

My dad passed away over thirty years ago. He was my hero growing up, the breadwinner and ultimate caregiver for our family. When he became ill, it was shocking, as he had always been in remarkable health. He exuded such vibrancy in everything he did. He loved playing practical jokes and relished telling a good story, whether it was 100 percent true or not—and it was usually not. He was quite handsome, with a full face, mischievous eyes, and the most beautiful hair. I nicknamed him the Silver Fox when he was in his late fifties because of his thick, silvery hair.

My parents on their 25th wedding anniversary

He didn't smoke, he didn't drink; he played tennis and kept extremely fit. He worked hard all his life—long strenuous days for over thirty-one years as a jet mechanic for TWA—and finally retired. It should have been a glorious time lasting many decades. But only a few years into retirement, he started to have significant health issues, noticeably aging decades in the course of a year.

As he deteriorated and health decisions needed to be made, my mother became his full-time caregiver. Their plans for retirement travel quickly faded. Sadly, they had put travel off, thinking they'd have time once my dad retired. They were excited, planning to use my dad's lifetime retiree airline pass to go wherever they wanted. But that wasn't to be.

Bragging about his latest tennis conquests changed to discussions about his increasing symptoms and failing health. I vividly recall how both my parents were in disbelief and denial over my dad's rapid decline, and unfortunately, his condition would never improve. It wasn't long before the entirety of their lives together became a strict list of daily—hourly—caregiving to-dos. Soon, there were no future plans beyond making it through another dreary day.

My mom becoming my dad's caregiver was odd if you knew my parents. She was incredibly petite, fragile, and nine years older than my father. If you'd asked most people, they might have thought my dad—a tall and incredibly strong man for most of his life—would end up caring for my frail little mom.

As his illness worsened, there were many 911 calls, falls, and other miseries. After many failed in-home care scenarios, my mother finally placed him in a nursing home. He hated that nursing home, and it felt to me that he hated us for putting him there.

At the time, I was pregnant and then a first-time mom. I worked full-time and was overwhelmed with time constraints and parenting responsibilities. For my dad, that meant infrequent visits from his only daughter, and even fewer from an out-of-state son. He had my mother, who was devoted to him and spent nearly every day with him. But even with her dedication and support, every day was impossibly dark. His decline felt cruel and unfair. His final days were almost unbearably sad. He'd die in that nursing home.

At the nursing home with their two-week-old grandson

He was such a great father and provider for our family. He ought to have lived into his nineties. My two sons deserved to spend decades with him. He was supposed to get the chance to teach his mechanical skills to his grandsons. And if he had to die so young, I wish he could have gone more quickly and painlessly, and not in a nursing home he despised. His final days should have allowed him some sense of privacy and dignity. I wish he could have died in his own bed, in the comfort of his home.

But even with death, life goes on. Suddenly, my mother was no longer a caregiver. She lived for some sixteen additional years, almost half of that on her own.

I helped her navigate a new life without my father. They were married for forty-seven years, and his absence, at such an early age, was a staggering blow to her. He was the CEO and more of the household. His death meant a lot of changes and challenges. My role as a daughter faded, morphing into that of my mother's caregiver. Actually, my entire family—including our young kids—became her caregiving team. Mom eventually moved in and lived with us for nine years before she passed away at the age of ninety-three.

Now, it's hard to believe she has been gone for fifteen years; it feels more recent. I miss both of my parents so much. Writing this book has been challenging.

I remember Mom's final weeks of hospice. Together, we planned her funeral. We shared—numerous times and with many tears—our admiration, respect, and love for each other. We said our goodbyes repeatedly. We held hands, something we didn't typically do on a normal day. Then, one day, she went to sleep and didn't wake up. She would be in a coma for a week, frail and unresponsive.

She was ready to die. You would have thought that the final week might be easier, knowing she was at peace. Her advanced age and declining health should have made it easier. But it wasn't easy. I came to learn that someone dying—even an anticipated death—is hard for those who will soon be left behind. No matter how much mental preparation went into it, holding her hands in her final moments—anxiously listening for her final breaths—was emotionally and spiritually jarring. At least for me.

She received no nourishment for a week, and though her doctor wasn't sure if my mom was in pain, her body involuntarily twitched as she wasted away. So, I regularly inserted a dropper full of morphine and whatever water I could get her to swallow between her peeling dry lips. I wasn't going to allow her to suffer.

While I desperately pleaded with God to take her, I also held on tightly to her hand and didn't want to let go. I felt such conflict. I knew she wanted to go; I knew her body was ready to stop. But while I prayed for her to pass quickly, I secretly hoped she might wake up, even if for a single moment. I wanted one more goodbye, one more "I love you."

But she didn't wake up, and remained in that coma for seven days before she died. Seven days of watching her body shut down. Seven days of pleading and bargaining with her to simply let go. And then, finally, she did.

I think about both my parents often. It saddens me that, as I get older, memories become harder to pull up from the increasingly distant past. I can still see my dad as if I'm looking at a still photograph, but previously memorable instances have faded. It's hard to remember his voice, his mannerisms, and the moments we shared. I sometimes talk to him, telling him I'm sorry if I let him down during his final year of life spent in the misery of that nursing home.

He was supposed to live a longer life and enjoy his retirement. Decades of hard work likely killed him. As an airline mechanic back then, he was exposed to serious toxins every day. All of his crew died young, probably because of those toxins. I think about his age when he died, only sixty-eight. I'll soon be sixty-eight myself, yet I feel young. I wonder if that's how he felt, like he had decades ahead of him.

He never answers me when I talk to him. I never feel him nearby. I hope that is because so much time has passed.

I still feel my mother's presence, although that too is fading with time. I talk to her sometimes, usually when stressed or challenged, or when I feel sad, lonely, or overwhelmed. When I talk to her now, I am not her caregiver. I go back to our daughter/mother role, when she was my family's caregiver. "Mom, please help me. Mom, what should I do? Mom, I miss you." I can almost hear her whisper, "Just take a breath; everything will work out." I feel her presence, especially when I'm out in the garden and a pink-throated hummingbird flits by.

I wish they both could have seen their grandsons grow into two wonderful young men; seen them graduate from high school and college; been proud of two Eagle Scouts. Many times, I said to my young sons, "My dad knew everything about that. I wish you could have known him. I wish he could have taught you that."

It's strange that my parents experienced such different caregiving journeys. He died quite young, in a nursing home, in sheer misery. She died in her nineties, at home, in relative peace.

The loss I experienced with their deaths was vastly different as well. When my dad died, I was not his day-to-day caregiver, my life didn't revolve around his care, as I was home with a newborn.

While I was tremendously sad at losing my father, I was also preoccupied and concerned about how my mother would survive the loss of her husband, and all that went with it. Dad was Mom's protector, companion, confidant, and dance partner. He was the bill-payer and the person who repaired things. He was involved in almost every aspect of her life. She loved him and relied on him for so many things. For him to be gone was scary for her, but also me. While I mourned him, I didn't have time to dwell on his loss; I needed to quickly step into his very big shoes and help my mom.

When Mom passed, however, I felt such immense loneliness and loss. I no longer had parents and was no longer a daughter. I was no longer a full-time caregiver, as I had been for so long. There was a loss of identity, purpose, and familiarity. The comfort of my daily priorities and habits had disappeared. My previously over-scheduled routine was immediately replaced by a sense of nothingness. Where was I supposed to be? What was I supposed to be doing?

I felt lost and I struggled. I also felt great guilt about any number of things. What had I done wrong? Could I have done more? The sense of loss worsened over time. It would be years before I felt whole again, and many more years before I could write about how affected I was by all of the loss.

You may be in the midst of your own caregiving journey, too. Or perhaps you will be in the future. What will unfold as you go down this new path? Will you discover you have a strength you weren't previously aware of? Will the time you spend caregiving result in an even deeper relationship with a loved one?

And while your blessings will be numerous and rewarding, what will be difficult for you? What will your stresses be? Will your new role be challenging for your career and family obligations? Will caregiving take a toll on your mental or physical health? How will it shape your interactions and future relationships with other family members?

Whether you are or will be a caregiver, you may also be thinking about your own caregiving needs in the future. I know I sometimes think about that. We hope and pray we won't lose our mental faculties. We want to be independent. We want to stay in our home. We don't want to become a burden. And while we likely think of our own future needs in that way, it is inevitable that at some point down the road, we will be a burden on someone who loves us. Who will that be? How will caregiving affect them and their family? What kind of journey will both you and they have as you need more help and care?

Unfortunately, no one can predict how a given caregiving story will unfold. Family dynamics, the duration of the caregiving role, the health status of the loved one, the life situation of the caregiver (children, career, finances, etc.), and so much more, all shape the path that each journey will take.

I can only share my mom's and dad's stories, and the narrative of the rewards and emotional scars of our combined caregiving journeys. Additionally, I interviewed more than a dozen other caregivers to share their experiences and insights as well.

I think my mother would be pleased that she inspired me enough to write these thoughts down. She had incredible strength and determination, both while caregiving for my father and while living with our family in her final years of life. She'd love that she and my dad—and so many other loved souls—are the focus of this book.

Chapter 2

Becoming a caregiver

There are only four kinds of people in the world. Those who have been caregivers. Those who are currently caregivers. Those who will be caregivers, and those who will need a caregiver.
Rosalyn Carter

After my father passed away, the next few weeks were spent honoring him as a loving husband, sibling, uncle, father, and grandfather. At the funeral, my husband read a letter I wrote. I couldn't read it. All I could do was stare at my grieving mom and sob. The funeral was so difficult. I had never lost someone close to me before. They say losing a family member is one of the most stressful events a person can endure. But there were many more stresses to come.

Who knew dealing with someone's death would be almost as painful as watching them die? After feeling the love from so many people at the funeral, after telling wonderful stories and sharing many beautiful memories, the warm feelings were quickly replaced by legal and financial matters, and endless paperwork.

No one seemed to care that I had lost my father; he was merely another claim to be dealt with. Every agency (banks, his insurance company, the IRS, etc.) had its forms and procedures. I referred to all of it as a pile of "proof of death paperwork," as all the companies seemed to care about was whether I could in fact prove my dad was truly deceased. Any expression of sympathy was impersonal and unfeeling. It was such a miserable and lengthy process, lasting a good part of a year before everything was finalized. I remember trying to stifle the sounds of my sniffling while on the phone with customer service reps. I don't know if I was crying because I was once again faced with telling someone my dad died, or out of sheer misery over the dreary and frustrating process.

Time passed and Mom was having a difficult time adjusting, specifically to being alone. Sure, she'd been *living* alone while my dad was in the nursing home, but she wasn't ever without his guidance. She had never been truly alone, as she'd spent most of her time with him at the nursing home. Now, she had a lot of time to dwell on his miserable end, and the years ahead without him as her guide and companion. She was also experiencing a lot of guilt over Dad not being home when he passed. Mom couldn't forgive herself for sending him to the nursing home. She was so sad that he died there. It was an emotional time for her; she and my dad were devoted lifetime companions.

Along with missing my dad, Mom seemed lost and disconnected. She had deprioritized keeping up with people while spending her days at the nursing home. In the initial months after Dad died, she became very isolated. Fortunately, my parents had a strong community of friends, and Mom had a longtime group of lady friends she had nicknamed, "The Lunch Bunch." She re-engaged with those friendships and seemed much more content about a year after Dad's passing.

While she was still driving locally, her Lunch Bunch friends met her at the nearby community center for lunch and other activities. Later, when she was no longer able to drive, one of them would pick her up. Somewhat by coincidence (my husband and I had attended the same high school, although we didn't meet until later), my mother-in-law lived only a few minutes away from my parents' home, so she was very helpful in bringing Mom out to our house for holidays, birthdays, and many activities in between. With their two young grandsons (I had a second son about a year after Dad passed), there were Easter egg hunts, Christmas festivities, and more to enjoy. They joined us on many trips to local parks, zoos, and other kid-friendly venues. I have dozens of family videos—recently transferred to digital form from old VHS tapes—showing both grandmothers enjoying their two lively grandsons. It was a fun and memorable time, although photos and videos from back then always remind me that Dad was already no longer with us.

Mom seemed to do okay in the family home for many years. I visited weekly to help her with whatever she needed help with. Usually, it was paperwork or something related to the house. Without her resident handyman (my dad could repair almost anything), the house seemed to be falling apart. We were always hiring someone to do something, although I tried my best to keep up with the home maintenance and the yard.

Even though she had friends that she did things with, we felt Mom was still isolated. She was home alone much of the time. She had to fix her own meals, and I worried that she wasn't eating well. I also didn't like the idea of her being in the house by herself in case something happened.

We talked a lot about what her next steps might be, what could make things easier for her, or help keep her engaged with others. Eventually, we made the decision to sell Mom's house and downsize to an apartment in a nearby retirement community. The apartment was not far from her old neighborhood, friends, and church. It seemed like a good plan.

For Mom, moving meant giving up the family home she had shared with my dad and raised our family in. Every inch of that home could have told so many wonderful stories about its occupants over the years. She was leaving those memories, longtime neighbors, and familiarity. We knew it would be stressful for her.

Her new apartment was very small. How does one move an entire life's worth of belongings from a three-bedroom home, into a tiny one-bedroom apartment? It wasn't easy. There were many days dedicated to sorting, discarding, and getting rid of treasured things. We made dozens of trips to local charities to let go of many "treasures," including encyclopedia sets, her paint-by-number paintings, numerous crafts, furniture, and so much more. I recall when we put my parents' very outdated lime-green couch out on the curb for garbage pickup after determining that no charity had wanted it. Mom called me in tears that day, describing how the couch was tossed into the garbage truck and unceremoniously crushed.

The apartment came with a small kitchen and a meal plan at a dining room within the complex. The retirement community was not a care facility; it wasn't a place for disabled

14

people or those with dementia. Residents needed to be healthy enough to walk around. It was actually nice that the residents were all mobile, as she met new friends she could do things with. She attended church and went on community outings, visiting museums, local gardens, and other venues. She took a few classes. I still recall getting her very first—perhaps her only—email when she took a class about how to use a personal computer.

She was in her early eighties, and while she had some "age-related" health issues and diminished vision, she was relatively healthy. She came across as very frail, but I think that was more due to her petite size and her thin, wispy gray hair. She had a clear mind and was still active. I loved that she regularly made it to lunches with her Lunch Bunch crowd.

She seemed content in her new home, and I tried to visit her at least once a week, which was about a thirty-minute drive. I paid her bills, did medical insurance paperwork and the like. I shopped with her, took her to the doctor and pharmacy, and kept tabs on her. Sometimes I'd have lunch with her at her apartment complex or elsewhere. I got to know some of her new neighbors and friends. We also spoke on the phone nearly every day.

The apartment arrangement—with my weekly visits and frequent phone calls—was working.

Truth #1: There's no such thing as a bullet-proof caregiving plan

Then, in a heartbeat, the arrangement screeched to a halt.

Actually, it was an issue of heartbeats that had created the problem. Mom had a heart attack.

I was at the ER and hospital so many times with my dad, and now I was back again with my mom—waiting, worrying, and praying. But she quickly stabilized. Mom, it seemed, was a very tough cookie under that sweet, delicate exterior.

A few days after being admitted to the hospital, a discharge nurse pushed a clipboard in my face. "Where are you going to take her to recuperate?" she asked. It was then I realized our existing caregiving plan did not provide for post-hospitalization recuperation. Mom needed to move someplace providing 24-hour care. So where was that going to be? The hospital suggested a nursing home. I suggested my family's home. Mom insisted on her apartment. I don't know why I didn't fight this at the time, maybe out of respect that she still wanted to be independent. Or perhaps it was sheer exhaustion after almost losing her. I can't remember. But home she went, back to her apartment, with a very tenuous plan for her care.

She wasn't supposed to be left alone at night, so I'd make the trip to her apartment, fix her dinner, and spend the night on her living room floor. A local cousin (thank you Susan) did the same a few nights. Mom could get around reasonably well in her tiny apartment, and we left meals in her fridge for the day. We were worried she'd have to move out if she couldn't get back on her feet soon. The retirement complex didn't allow residents to have food brought to their apartments from the dining room, and residents were supposed to be fully mobile. But my mom was determined to be "okay," and amazingly, she was very quickly up and around again. So, the post-health-emergency plan worked, at least for that time.

I don't know how she felt those days, if she was more concerned about dying or about living. I sometimes reflect on this now—was she scared she might go to a similar nursing home as my dad? She hated that place almost as much as he did. I think she recovered so quickly because she had a mission and sheer determination.

Her mission was to retain her independence and never go into a nursing home. She said more than once that she wanted to die in her own bed at home.

Truth #2: Prayer can in fact be part of the caregiving strategy

But within the year, there'd be another health emergency, and then another. It is all somewhat foggy for me now. I can only remember moments, most of them in hospital waiting rooms, usually pleading with God or nurses. Asking God not to take her, while trying to get a warm blanket or other comfort item from the nearest nurse.

And then, once, asking God to take her, as she was so sick and in such pain. But the Good Lord must have felt she still needed to be on this Earth. She recovered time and time again.

Mom was a gentle southern soul, and I often thought she got extra special care in the hospital. She was always so pleasant and appreciative. Nurses thought she was so sweet. She had the cutest little wrinkles. She'd hate that I told you that. She hated it when I or other people referred to her as "cute." But all she needed to do was demurely ask for something in her quiet southern drawl, and she'd have at least one nurse holding her hand and doing her bidding, while telling her what a little doll she was.

Mom also enjoyed what she lovingly referred to as her "southern prayer network"—dozens of relatives in the South who were putting in a good word for her up above. Considering how well she rebounded from her various hospital emergencies, I always did attribute prayer as one of her extended caregiving team's secret weapons.

Chapter 3

Facing a "new normal"

Over time, trips to my mom's apartment and to medical appointments—both planned and increasingly unplanned—became more and more frequent. I'd try to bring my two sons, but that didn't often work out well. The apartment was small, and there was nothing for two energetic young boys to do.

Mom and her two grandsons

Taking them with me was stressful, as they'd get into things or get too rowdy with each other. Mom sometimes bribed them to be good. My sons knew and loved her as their grandmother, and they enjoyed spending time with her at our house and other venues. But I don't believe they liked these visits to her apartment. They knew she was someone who distracted my attention from them, and it was also a lengthy trip back and forth (that usually wasn't focused on their having any fun).

Eventually, Mom's health-related needs began affecting my job. The unplanned interruptions were particularly challenging, but even the planned activities, like errands and medical appointments, increasingly started to cause stress on my work schedule.

Some of this schedule craziness was, I suppose, self-imposed. I had already developed that caregiver mentality of needing to do everything myself. Mom was no longer driving by this point. While she sometimes used the county's senior outreach transportation to get around to visit friends, and used the apartment complex's van to get to church, when she would suggest she take such transportation to a medical checkup, I would always firmly say "no." *I* wanted to take her and meet with every doctor. I maintained a list of questions and concerns, which we'd review with her doctor each visit. I know she was happy to have me take her and be her advocate, as well as keep track of medications and test results—not to mention insurance paperwork—but I know she always worried she was taking up too much of my time.

While having two children at home and helping out my mom, I tried to juggle the pickups, drop-offs, medical appointments, and the desire to "be there" for everyone. Working full-time went from challenging to impossible. I was lucky I had the option to reduce my hours. I know many caregivers can't do that due to finances or health insurance coverage, etc. My husband carried our medical insurance at the time, and we were financially stable even with a reduction in my income. I eventually switched to a part-time schedule, transitioning from a management position to an individual contributor role, and from an office to a cubicle—both of which were a jolt to my ego at the time.

This part-time schedule "kind of" worked… until one day, it didn't. Eventually, even working part-time in an office—and commuting to help my mom—was a struggle and I felt as if I was torn in too many directions. I talked to my husband, John, and we decided to ask Mom to move in with us. I thought I could do freelance consulting part-time from home, which would have made keeping an eye on her much easier. I would have had more flexibility too. It seemed like a good plan.

I asked her if she wanted to move in. I wasn't sure she'd want to, as she was always reluctant to "be a burden," as she used to say. Besides, our two sons were quite lively and a handful. But I barely finished the sentence before she said "Yes," and within a month, we moved her to our home and into our chaotic lives.

I didn't really think about it at the time, but now I realize that my husband had signed up to be a full-time caregiver—and to a degree, our young sons had as well.

Chapter 4

Expanding the nest

When Mom moved in with us, our sons were ages six and eight.

From a logistics standpoint, moving her into our home was not that hard. We had a guest room with its own bathroom; this room was separated from the rest of the house, and on the first floor. We outfitted her bathroom with a variety of disability equipment, including a shower grab bar and an elevated toilet seat with grab bars. I redecorated the guest bedroom just for her. She was always a pink rose fan, so I bought a bedroom sheet/comforter set adorned with beautiful pink roses. I hung up her pink rose artwork and even installed pink fixtures for the bathroom. Fluffy pink towels, too. It was fun to fix that room up for her. We were all excited to have her move in.

Not so fun was the move out of her apartment, which meant further consolidation of what she'd already downsized. I was amazed at how much we'd managed to fit in that tiny apartment. We separated her remaining belongings into four groups: a bedroom set and a few other possessions that fit in our home; items that went into storage; furniture that she gave away to friends at her apartment complex; and an ample amount of donations for charity.

Truth #3: Nothing you put into storage is worth keeping

Note to others: paying to store a bunch of excess stuff you're not likely to ever use again, is otherwise known as hoarding. If you really wanted it, you'd find room for it in your home.

We kept two antique sewing machines, odd pieces of furniture, and countless other "treasures" in storage for nine years. Let me pass on to you a major "aha" I learned as a result of this: calling something old an "antique" doesn't make it valuable or worth keeping.

Mom loved crafts, so there were some unique (and extremely large) items she had created, including a very tall resin lamp made of crushed green glass bits, and a coffee table made of colorful tiles. There was no place for them in our home, yet we didn't want her to have to part with them. The funny thing is that she would never have known, or probably cared, if we'd donated them. In retrospect, it was more about *my* concerns over getting rid of *her* things.

I'd hate to calculate the storage cost for all those years, and most everything ended up discarded after Mom passed away. The few things I kept, including one of the "antique" sewing machines and some framed artwork, I tucked away in closets until we recently downsized ourselves. Those items found new homes after my clinging to them for so many years.

As I look now at the few inherited items I did hang on to, I've realized my sons likely won't want a bunch of my parents' old stuff either. So, what will happen with the family heirlooms, including precious handmade pieces like my mom's quilts and embroidery? Then there's my dad's military memorabilia, old family photos, and other collectibles. And let's not forget the family china and elegant tableware that I haven't even used since Mom passed away. I recently asked one son if he'd want his grandmother's sterling silver, and he asked, "Well, what's it worth?"

I don't think there's a lot they'd want from my generation of treasures either. Now I'm hoping for at least one daughter-in-law who might appreciate family heirlooms for the stories they tell versus their worth if sold.

Chapter 5

Sandwiches and fishbowls

The day the roles reverse is foreign. It's a clumsy dance of love and responsibility, not wanting to cross any lines of respect. It's honoring this person who gave their life to you—not to mention literally gave you life—and taking their fragile body in your hands like a newborn, tending to their every need.
Lisa Goich-Andreadis

I was in my early forties when my mom moved in with our young family, and I thought about what our new multigenerational household might mean to our everyday lives. I knew there'd be some juggling to meet everyone's needs and schedule. But I really thought it would be better than the long-distance care plan we'd been struggling with.

Little did I know, I was now part of a large and growing community of caregivers who were living their lives "sandwiched" between caring for an aging parent and raising their children or grandchildren. I learned that multigenerational families were becoming the norm versus the exception. Between the aging population, women having kids later, young adults moving back into the nest, and elders moving in with their adult children, more than half of Americans in their forties were finding themselves in such a sandwich.[3]

This trend has only continued with today's younger generations (particularly people born between 1965 and 1996) taking on about 80 percent of so-called "sandwich caregiving." With some 10,000 baby boomers (people born between 1946 to 1964) reaching retirement age every day—many with chronic medical conditions and long-term care needs—the demand for sandwich family caregivers will only increase.[4]

We welcomed Mom into our lively Blum sandwich, with high hopes it would work out. She loved the rose-themed room and was truly appreciative. I recall feeling a little anxious that first day, but once she was moved in, having her there quickly became very familiar. The only change for me—at least on the surface—was meal planning. I needed to be more regimented, as her diet had some specific needs. Previously, our family had resorted to fast food at least weekly as we ran from one kid function to the next. Once my mom moved in, I tried to reduce the frequency and aimed to always have a healthy meal on the table. I wasn't really someone who loved cooking, so I did have to up my game.

By this time, Mom was deemed legally blind, having had progressive macular degeneration for many years. She could see, but only with the strongest prescription glasses. She needed to be close to things, so we set up her La-Z-Boy chair a few feet from her TV. We also had every visual aid you could think of, including a phone with enormous numbered buttons, a clock that spoke the time out loud, etc.

The kids quickly developed a much closer relationship with her, and loved that their Granny (what our family called her most of the time) was living with us. They often helped her find things or use her technology, like the telephone answering machine or TV remote. I may never know what all they conned her into doing or approving, but I would sometimes leave the kids with her for short periods of time. I used to tell people that she was watching them, but they were also watching her.

I don't really know how Mom felt about her new life and home back then. She regularly and sincerely thanked my husband and me for all we did for her. She would tell our kids

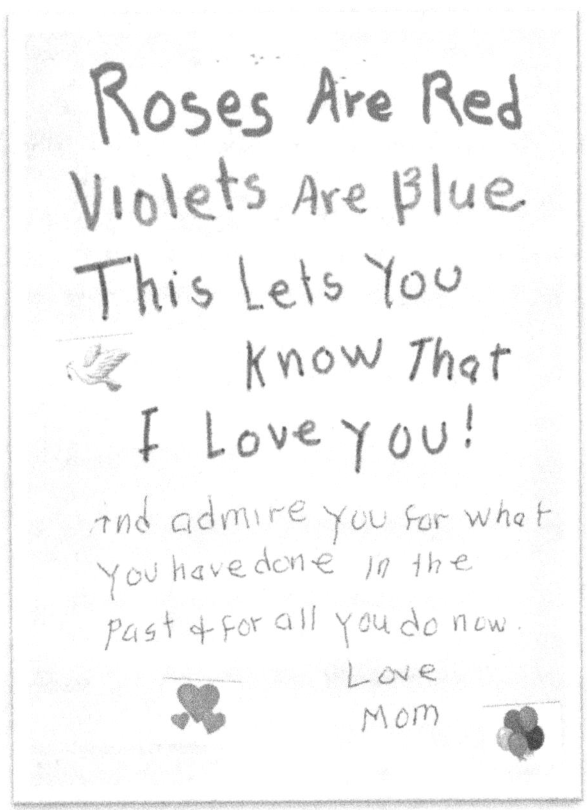

that their mom had to spend a lot of energy on them and on her, so they should be nice to me. She often told us, or the kids, how much she hated to be a bother. I still have dozens of sweet notes she wrote to thank us for caring for her.

I did hear from other people, like her friends and our relatives, that she was happy, but I am guessing there were many things she simply accepted. Our boys were high-energy and loud; our lives were chaotic, and our schedules were demanding. I think another person might have registered some complaints, but she never did. Suffice it to say there was some adjustment necessary, but the arrangement did work. Mom seemed happy, and I could keep an eye on her, take her to her appointments, and keep her engaged. The kids were getting to know her; it was heartwarming to see them grow closer.

While I was focusing on our sons and my mom, my poor husband wasn't getting much attention, but he agreed she needed to live with us, something I have always appreciated. John genuinely seemed to enjoy having Mom around, and they developed a friendly relationship with some mutual teasing (usually about me) always at the forefront.

Everyone was clicking. Three generations were managing.

True, life in a sandwich could get very overwhelming when Mom was having a health issue. It wasn't simply the stress on my schedule and the family schedule, it was the anxiety an unexpected health event would cause. There were times after her recovery from heart-related problems or other health episodes, that I feared I was going to walk into our house and find her dead on the floor.

Along with living in a sandwich, the other adjustment was living in a fishbowl of sorts. A fishbowl? Yes, you become highly visible to the outside world. When you live with someone who is elderly or disabled, *their* life becomes what is happening in *your* life. Your life becomes their topic of conversation with family and friends.

You walk by your loved one's room and hear your life being retold on the phone. Something happened this morning with one of your sons, and you hear the rehash of it at 3 p.m. Your life is the news, and every time you turn around, a reporter is showing the world all of your successes and, more importantly, all of your defeats. The defeats seemed to get more coverage—just like in the news—after all, the bad things are what pique everyone's interest.

One son didn't do well on an important test. Another was playing games on the internet and was being punished. Diane was stressed out about something happening with a client. A door was repeatedly slammed the previous night, with no explanation. Diane would be having a colonoscopy tomorrow. Each and every detail of my life would be played out multiple times in my mom's phone conversations, because what else did she have to talk about? Her phone became her lifeline. Her daily observations about life were limited. And so, the featured topic of the day was always, *"What are the Blums up to today?"*

Living in a fishbowl means you are visible and made public, and most people aren't comfortable feeling that exposed. Usually, we can hide aspects of our lives we don't want the world to hear about. I'm not saying my life was full of illegal, immoral, or terrible things. But would most of us want our parenting skills, health status, or good ole family gossip discussed with people we don't know? Or even people we do? It bothered me sometimes.

Additionally, back living with a parent again—after a lifetime of being on my own—resulted in me feeling slightly judged at times. No, I'm not a very good cook. Yes, we went to McDonalds *again* to get the Happy Meal toy the boys didn't have. Yes, I let our youngest talk me into getting him a kitten even after I firmly said it was never going to happen.

But hey, I'm a good mom, Mom!

Fishbowls and sandwiches. Interesting analogies for my family's life. Both have good aspects to them. If I weren't in a fishbowl back then, my mom wouldn't have been with us.

Sandwiches are delicious and sustain you. Having multiple generations in one home is something special. As Dr. Cabeca mentioned in her foreword for this book, there has been research showing that multigenerational households provide health benefits and help promote longevity in all members of the household. There were many other wonderful benefits to my family, as well. My kids weren't close to my mom before she had moved in with us; after she moved in, they bonded with her and got to know her quite well. They definitely have many more stories about me and my childhood that she shared with them, creating a sense of legacy and family roots, even though my kids had few relatives in their daily lives.

They have also now lived with an elderly person, and I can only hope it helps them appreciate the fragileness of older people as they come across them in the world. I jokingly say I am glad they have been shown how important it is to care for "their old mom" someday, too.

So, we lived our lives, sandwiched in our fishbowl, for nine years. My husband laughed a lot about our fishbowl lives. It didn't faze him like it sometimes bothered me. But he left the fishbowl every day, and commuted to work and a life of his own, so he didn't quite live the experience as I did.

Over the years, especially as my mom came to depend on me more and more, I found respite right outside the fishbowl—in my garden. Puttering around in the garden provided me a physical and mental break that truly recharged me.

For years, Mom joined me there, too. She'd either cut some roses, pull a few weeds, or simply sit out in the sun for a time. She loved all the hummingbirds and the pretty flowers. She enjoyed the dozens of wind chimes and whimsical decorations. I remember she'd proudly give tours of the garden to her friends when they came to visit. We'd sometimes chat while I gardened, but it was mainly simply a time of solitude for both of us. No medical appointments, no schedules, no caregiving to-dos.

At some point, she started to come out less and blamed it on her allergies or our windy backyard. I never really thought about it but now, thinking back, I hope she didn't feel I needed the space to myself; although, truthfully, I loved having a place where I could simply be in my head for a while.

Today, over a decade after my mom's passing, I still find peace and solitude in my garden; and when I'm there, I think of her. When we recently moved, I was sad to leave both the house Mom shared with us as well as the garden she enjoyed, and I actively encouraged her "spirit" to travel the seven-hour drive with us to our new home and garden.

Fishbowls and sandwiches. When you become a caregiver, things are going to change. Yes, you feel honored to be in such an important role and see how your efforts each day so positively affect your loved one. But you may sometimes have negative thoughts. Perhaps you desire greater flexibility, or maybe you are suffering from stress or fatigue due to multiple generations requiring your focus and energies. Perhaps you long for greater privacy.

For the most part, I adjusted to what each day would bring to all of us. Mom adjusted. My husband and sons adjusted. But once in a while, I felt "stuck" in the sandwich. Where was the "me time"? Why couldn't I plan a week and have it work out according to plan?

As I moved forward in my "new normal," I often journaled about life's blessings and challenges, my feelings, my frustrations, and many stressful and humorous stories I didn't want to forget. I have always found writing to be cathartic and calming. In my writings, I reflected on many beautiful moments I shared with Mom out in the garden and in our home. But I also captured moments of caregiver stress, for sure. Writing helped me gain perspective at times when I was overwhelmed.

I look back at my notes now, and am shocked to see how I truly felt some days. It is interesting that caregivers often suppress the memories of the bad days. I think it is like giving birth; if it was a difficult delivery, you forget about the pain in time to want to have that second child. Maybe it's nature's way of keeping us engaged with our loved ones even when it's challenging.

I remember the exact circumstances that prompted one particular journal entry. I came home from buying a bunch of flowers. I was happy and energized, as I was volunteering in one of my son's elementary school classes, teaching the kids different types of art. That day, we were going to paint watercolors. I planned to put the flowers on the kids' desks so they could study and paint them. I walked into the house with my arm full of flowers, and boom—my entire day became very different and frightening.

I saw Mom lying on the floor. She was semi-conscious, and I wasn't sure if she had experienced a problem prior to falling (like a heart attack), or had fallen and hurt herself. I immediately called 911. The fire department and ambulance arrived moments later, six enormous men in full gear carrying medical equipment. Even with me watching from the hallway outside the door, there was barely an inch of spare space in her room. They checked her vitals and put her on oxygen. Her vitals weren't good, so she was whisked off in the ambulance, with me following in my car.

It took hours to get an update on her status. I felt lightheaded as I sat and then paced in the waiting room. A major health incident was a resident fear in the back of my mind. Flashbacks of my dad being wheeled away to the nursing home swirled in my head. I couldn't push away those memories of his health deterioration costing him his home. "God, please don't let that happen to Mom. Please let her be okay."

I walked up to the nurse's station for a status update, at the same time the doctor finally came out. Yes, she had another heart attack, but was stable and doing well. When the doctor told me she would be okay I felt such a rush of relief. I finally exhaled. She'd soon be released and back home.

I brought the local firehouse a platter of cookies, thanking them for their help. It wasn't the first time that firehouse had helped us out, nor the last. Our daily routine kicked back in.

But after that, my mind never truly relaxed. I went into a hyper-vigilant mode. That "when is the other shoe going to drop?" feeling became one of the hardest things for me as her caregiver and daughter. Sometimes it did get to me.

**Diane's journal:
A seltzer bottle ready to blow**

Yesterday I cried. This is something I seem to do more these days. I guess you could put it down to middle-age hormonal changes or something, but more likely, it is because I am trapped in a sandwich. On one side is my family: my two teenage boys and their father. On the other side is my mom.

I love them all. It is so wonderful that my kids get to know my mom. It is so wonderful to be here for her.

But what about me? What about John?

I feel like I am so focused on keeping the sandwich together. Yet I often feel like I am the thing that is falling apart.

My days are not my own. My day's plan usually gets preempted by life. A child gets sick. A phone call from the school requires my attention. I walk in the door and my mother is calling out for help. I stay pretty calm and do what I need to do as these emergencies unfold. Then, in the quiet of night or alone in the laundry room, I cry. I look at myself and see someone tired and growing increasingly negative and overwhelmed.

People tell me I need to find an outside solution for my elderly mom. Translation: move her to a nursing home or other care facility. My mom even tells me that sometimes, after one of her health issues erupts, although I don't believe for even one second that is what she wants.

She is legally blind, but she is not blind to what is happening to me. She sees my stress. She sees my frustrations. I try to hide it all, but each day that passes, more of me is unable to keep it bottled up. I feel like a seltzer bottle that gets shaken up each day. Boy, someday I'm going to explode, and that is a bit scary sometimes.

Just when I feel like I can manage it all, maybe it has been a week of making progress on my various "to-do" lists, I will come home to an emergency. A heart attack, maybe. A call to 911, a trip to the hospital; the weariness of all that follows.

What else can I do? I love my mom and don't want her to be miserable and alone in a nursing home. We also love having her with us. But it is hard. She understands she is more work for me, but I don't think she truly understands the impact that she has on me sometimes, and I wouldn't tell her, it would crush her.

I never said anything to my mom about these feelings, and they'd usually go away after the particular "event" that triggered the negative feelings in the first place. Typically, the trigger had something to do with the state of her health, so not her fault in any case.

Chapter 6

More important truths about caregiving

I learned a lot about caregiving over the many years my mom lived with us. That experience, along with interviewing other caregivers while preparing this book, has given me a number of insights into some of the additional truths that come with the "job."

I'm sure that if you are in the middle of your own caregiving journey, many of these will resonate with you. If you haven't yet started your journey, I hope these insights will help prepare and inspire you.

Truth #4: Not everyone has the "caregiver gene"

To care for those who once cared for us is one of the highest honors.
Tia Walker

I can't really say when Mom became dependent on me and I transitioned from simply being a doting daughter to her caregiver. And as I talk to other caregivers, many have said the same thing. They aren't sure when or why they became "the one." They simply took on the role of caring for one or more parents a little at a time, even when there were other siblings in the picture—offering a little assistance here, a little paperwork there, followed by creeping losses of a loved one's independence, and one medical crisis after another.

Of course, sometimes the loved one is a spouse, and several people have shared their stories relating to dementia creeping into their partner's everyday life. A forgotten name, a lost pair of glasses, and then one day, others start to notice things. Many times, a person gets so used to their spouse's little memory blips that they unconsciously start to assist, filling in gaps during a story being told, or laughing off a tip-of-the-tongue moment. Then comes the realization that something more may be happening—and just like that, a diagnosis and a whole new journey begins.

Only a few people I spoke with were suddenly plunged into their caregiving role after a catastrophic medical event. In one instance, this was brought on by a stroke.

But in thinking about it, there must be a *reason* a given person becomes a caregiver of a parent as opposed to, let's say, their sibling taking on the role, or at least sharing it.

Some people have told me they believe there is a "caregiving gene" and that this gene shows up more in daughters than sons. I believe this to be true as well. Perhaps that's because the daughter/mom story is my story. But throughout my life, I've also seen that many of my female friends were—or still are—devoted caregivers.

I've often felt· women possess innate caregiving capabilities. Women are the moms after all. They have the babies. So, could motherhood or some sort of instinctual nurturing affect one's caregiving ability? I'm not sure. All I know is that daughters do more often seem to have "the gene." Interestingly, of the people I interviewed, a few daughters-in-law took on the role of caring for their in-laws, rather than their husband (the care receiver's son) assuming the responsibility.

I know I've always felt a strong inclination to help out and credit both of my parents for that caring attitude. They definitely gave me the gene. *But wait*! I was adopted as a baby, so my mom and dad were not my biological parents. There's no inherited gene in my case, if one in fact exists. So, when I talk about someone having (or not having) the caregiving gene, I'm not talking about biology. Instead, I'm referring to how they were brought up, something called *family scripts*. Family scripts are the expectations and values that are passed down within families and communities—they may include beliefs such as those relating to childcare, eldercare, and family responsibilities. They are learned from early childhood experiences, a family's culture, and social relationships.

In my and my older brother's baby boomer generation, family scripts were still predominantly rooted in the idea that women were the primary care providers for their children and parents. Thus, a female sibling would *more likely* take on caring for an elderly parent than a male sibling.

In my case, my brother (my only sibling) lived on the opposite coast and had life circumstances (he was divorced with kids) that made taking on—or even helping with—our mother's care impossible. But he probably wouldn't have become our mom's caregiver anyway, as our family script didn't set the expectation that he, a male, would ever take on the caregiving role for his parents—at least, not unless I (the female child) didn't for some reason. Sometimes a female sibling may lack a viable living situation (such as sufficient living space in the home, close proximity to a parent's home, flexibility at work, etc.), the financial means, or the mental fortitude to become the primary caregiver for mom or dad.

As a baby boomer, I was exposed to the script of my generation. Since then, the world has seen a tremendous shift in attitudes towards women. The fact that I worked full-time outside the home, while also being a mom, demonstrates how much my family script had evolved since my parents started our family back in the 1950s.

Such changes in generational attitudes may help explain the more recent increase seen in the male caregiver population.[5] Throughout their lives, Gen X (born in 1965-1980) and Millennial (born in 1981-1996) males were exposed to different values and expectations about parenting responsibilities compared to the young males of my generation. Gen X dads subsequently took on a more active role in caring for their kids. Their wives or partners probably worked full-time. Their family was possibly multigenerational, with these fathers more likely to be actively engaged in a sandwiched caregiving role. Now, *their* kids are receiving an ever-evolving family script reflecting today's views on parenting, childcare, and caregiving.

Cultural norms and expectations are part of family scripts, with some cultures partially dictating who should take on the caregiving responsibility—regardless of whether anyone else is willing (or the designated individual wants to). As an example, historically in traditional Japanese culture, it was assumed the eldest son's wife would take on the responsibility of caring for her husband's aging parents.[6] This viewpoint (aka family script), however, has been changing in modern times, although today's generation of elders may still believe it to be the norm. My husband (an only son) and I were the primary care providers for his Japanese mother for decades, but with our recent move, that role transitioned to a local sibling, his sister.

When we sold our family home, many of the people who put offers on it were planning on multigenerational households. One family had an elderly parent moving in with them. Another wanted to have two elderly parents—one each from both the husband's and wife's side—move in with them, along with their teenage daughter (a sandwiched living situation). I don't believe this arrangement was financially required, but instead was simply a plan for eldercare. Some people refer to this as "upsizing," or purchasing a new home larger than your core family needs, in order to accommodate parents or returning kids. About a third of U.S. adults in multigenerational homes say caregiving is a major reason for such a living arrangement, with 25 percent of those specifically citing adult caregiving as the need.[7]

Having divorced and/or remarried parents can add further complexities to who takes on their future care.[8] Sometimes stepsiblings are asked to "step up" to care for a non-biological parent. My father-in-law had remarried, and when his second wife died, his local adult stepchildren invited him into their home to live out his days. You never know how such relationships may play out when it comes to caregiving. I know of one woman who helped with her stepmom's caregiving, only to have no help from that mom's biological children when she later needed help for her biological father.

It's also possible that someone is thrust into the role against their will or desire—or perhaps someone may feel obligated to care for a spouse (even an ex-spouse) or relative if no one else steps up. About half of caregivers caring for a spouse/partner indicate they had no choice.[9] One woman I interviewed was considering divorcing her spouse before he was diagnosed with Alzheimer's. But she decided to remain in the marriage and became her husband's primary caregiver.

While I am fairly confident I got the caregiving gene through the caring attitudes of my parents and extended family (our family script), I also believe there may be a genetic influence, even if one hasn't been identified yet. Think about the character traits that are required of a caregiver: empathy and trust, having an ability to better deal with stress, and being open and caring, are a few examples. These "caregiving" traits could someday be found to be linked to a gene or genes.

There has already been some interesting research on this topic. One study suggested some caregiving traits may be linked to a gene involved with the hormone oxytocin. Oxytocin is often called the "hormone of love or bonding." In the study, people having certain variants of an oxytocin receptor gene were found to have better social skills and personality traits helpful to caregivers.[10] Of course, even if this oxytocin receptor gene does have some influence, there are often other genes and environmental factors that can modify the resulting behaviors. So, while influential, scientists believe life experiences (aka family scripts) presumably play a larger role.

At least today, daughters do more often seem to have the gene, although that is changing. Statistics support that the number of male caregivers is growing, whether it be due to evolving family scripts, genetics, or perhaps even today's shrinking family size (family size reduction means fewer potential caregivers for a given care receiver; sometimes there isn't a daughter). According to data from the National Alliance for Caregiving and AARP, some 16 million men were caregiving in 2015. That increased to 18.7 million in 2020.[11] More men can also be found caring for partners with dementia, as about twice as many women have the condition. Several men I interviewed for this book were the partners and caregivers of women with Alzheimer's disease, and I know from hearing their stories they all definitely had the gene.

A lot of factors go into who becomes a caregiver for a particular person. Love, duty, purpose, proximity, flexibility, the financial means, and other family obligations, to name a few. Each situation is unique.

It's also worth stating that not everyone should become a caregiver. Some, whether female or male, won't have the patience. Others won't have the kindness factor. Some may not be able to laugh at the many difficult moments. Sometimes people may have their own health or family priorities that simply make it impossible for them to take on caregiving for someone else. The list of potential reasons is long.

So, it is okay for someone (*including you*) to say they need to take a pass if they believe their temperament or life situation is not compatible with becoming someone's caregiver. Better to say, "I can't do it," than to go down a road you are certain you can't traverse. Just don't create roadblocks for the person who does step up, and also please offer them help along the way.

I do also realize that this level of self-awareness, as well as the ability to honestly communicate ("I can't do it") within one's family, is not always present. Some may step up to the caregiving role when they really shouldn't, for any number of reasons. In those cases, it's even more important that others try to support both the caregiver and the loved one. My mom used to say, "The best life happens when there is a village of care." If you aren't the caregiver, *become part of the village.*

Truth #5: Family and friends are your first line of support; let them know what you need

Sometimes asking for help is the bravest move you can make.
You don't have to go it alone.
Unknown

I didn't care for my mom alone. Believe me. My husband helped with whatever he could, and also helped me see things through a different—perhaps more positive—lens when need be. I found out early on that as a caregiver, you sometimes need to distort reality to get through a given day. Our sons also became co-caregivers very quickly and naturally.

I had numerous friends to lean on. Many of them were also in the midst of caregiving in some capacity, for one or both parents. I was blessed with a strong support system within my mom's and dad's extended families; I had prayers and positive words for me, and a social outlet for Mom.

My mother-in-law (thanks Gramma) was also nearby and, at least when our boys were young, was physically able to offer some assistance caring for them when I was focused elsewhere. She also developed a friendly relationship with my mom, and visited her from time to time.

It helped that Mom's health transitioned slowly over the nine years she lived with us. Although there were many crisis moments in hospitals along the way, she always—somewhat remarkably—rebounded quite well. In general, she lived a happy and comfortable life, with a very slow "deterioration" over her time with us. She never lost her mental capacities, for which I am extremely thankful.

She was also a kind and loving soul, very easy to get along with. She had a sweet disposition and an ability to laugh at things that others might have opted to become bitter about. She used to say, "That's water off a duck's back. No use fretting about things you can't change."

Most of the people I interviewed for this book had family and friends as their primary support team. Many, like me, incorporated their kids into caregiving roles. Assistance from neighbors, church affiliations, and other community support was also often used. Very few actually included professional care (in-home care, nursing homes, etc.) until very late in their caregiving journey, if at all.

In my own case, my husband and sons provided me with coverage when I needed to be away, and gave me a little respite and flexibility. During the earlier years Mom lived with us, we could even safely leave her for a few days. We'd alert neighbors (thank you Roy and Julie, Gary and Kathy, and many others) who looked in on her, and she had their numbers on speed dial. I remember she called them from time to time, and I so appreciated their willingness to stop by and help her. Usually, it was a question relating to some form of technology, like a TV remote she couldn't get to work.

Her friends, of course, were awesome at keeping in touch with her and taking her out when she was still up for that. They'd go to a community center and have lunch, listen to music, and sometimes even line dance. It was fortunate that one of the Lunch Bunch members lived out near our house, so it was convenient for her to take Mom the thirty-minute drive to and from these outings (appreciated your kindness, Sylvia). My mother had a lot of fun with this group of friends. She'd usually come home exhausted, but with many funny stories and some new gossip to share. It also got her out of the Blum fishbowl so that she had other things to talk about with her relatives on the phone.

Members of the Lunch Bunch

We found an agency for the blind who sent an outreach specialist (thank you Carolyn) to visit each week. She brought many helpful visual aids, including audio books, for Mom. The two became quite friendly, and my mom looked forward to those visits.

She was constantly chatting on the phone, and a number of our relatives went out of their way to keep in frequent touch with her. My cousin Susan came and spent time with her, too. In the earlier years, they often went for lunch or afternoon tea. The beautiful photo of Mom at the end of the book, was taken by Susan at one such outing. I laugh now as I think that during some of this time, my mom enjoyed a more active social life than I did.

I remember instances where Mom suggested I check her in for a weekend at one of the local retirement homes or nursing homes that offered temporary caregiving support to the elderly, to provide respite to their caregiver. She brought this up multiple times as an idea to give me some "time off." She obviously saw signs of wear and tear that I wasn't acknowledging myself. I was never open to taking her to one of these. It seemed very extreme to me, to take her out of her comfy environment and routine simply so I and/or my family could get away from her. In retrospect, a little respite, especially later on when my family wasn't able to leave her to go on vacations, might have been a healthy thing for all of us, and I'm sure she would have been okay.

Respite is an area where siblings who aren't otherwise able to help (or have chosen not to) can be enlisted, like an out-of-town sibling coming to stay for a week while you take a vacation. Most of the caregivers I spoke with didn't focus on respite—or if they did, it was tough for them to figure out a workable plan. This is so unfortunate, as it's a wonderful way for caregivers to take a break and reconnect with core family members that may be feeling neglected. In Mom's final few years, my brother Pat (thanks bro) came out to stay with her, as did an out-of-state cousin, Cornelia (thanks dear). My mom's East Coast granddaughters (love you Jenny and Melissa) visited a few times as well, and were good at connecting with her on the phone.

Granny and her granddaughters in our backyard

It is imperative that you surround yourself with family and friends as a primary line of support. Ask people for *specific* help—sometimes they won't understand what you may be struggling with most. Maybe you need someone to go grocery shopping or gas up your car. Perhaps you need help catching up with household chores like laundry. Or you may simply need someone to sit with your loved one while you take a break. Most family and friends are happy to help out if they know what they're signing up for.

Be sensitive, though, to the fact that there can sometimes be challenges within this intimate caregiving community. Good communication is key.

Truth #6: Family relationships may be affected

While I don't think my caregiving role and decision-making negatively affected any family relationships, I did hear this as a common theme from others. When a loved one starts to lose their independence, when decisions have to be made, and when "someone" steps up to make those decisions, family relationships can become strained. Out-of-town relatives may not understand the deteriorated state of a loved one's physical or mental health, so they may interject inappropriate wishes or demands. Siblings may not agree with a parent's care plan or how finances are being spent. Even the evolving relationship between caregiver and care receiver can become difficult.

We were fortunate, as I had already been helping Mom, so it wasn't a huge transition when she moved in with my family. I didn't have to "take over" a lot of things that I hadn't already been helping with, like bill paying and activities relating to medical appointments and her health (prescriptions, etc.). Additionally, my relationship with her was still very much mom and adult daughter, versus the primary focus being her caregiver, for many years—allowing us to get comfortable in our transitioning roles. My brother was appreciative, and relatives were supportive.

Most of the people I interviewed spoke of issues with siblings, both the caregiver's siblings and the siblings of the care receiver. The caregiver's siblings were often absent from the caring arrangement, weren't helpful, or became at odds with caregiving decisions. Many issues were grounded in financial and inheritance concerns.

The care receiver's siblings were typically out-of-town relatives who were questioning decisions or perhaps feeling the need to be more intimately involved in some way. I do recall a few relatives visiting over the many years my mom lived with us, and sometimes feeling they were doing some polite sleuthing to ensure Mom was being treated like a queen (as she was, of course).

Besides these problems, a caregiver may face difficulties within their own core family. A spouse may feel neglected, or have financial concerns about caregiving costs or related income reductions. Children may simply want more of their caregiving parent's attention. The fact that these relationships may become deprioritized—even if slightly and unintentionally—is an important point many caregivers (including me) said they sometimes overlooked or took for granted. Caregivers can start to view themselves and prioritize their lives based on their responsibilities as a caregiver, rather than their role as a wife, husband, partner, mother, father, friend, employee, etc. This is especially true over time as the requirements for caregiving increase.

In my case, my husband and children were very open to my mom moving in with us. I'm not sure they thought it would affect them very much. But I do think it did. There were many positive effects, of course. But there were some adverse effects as well. Not immediately, but over time, my primary focus became more and more that as Mom's caregiver. There was always a "let me check with Granny" comment before scheduling any new commitments or even leaving the house. Sometimes it meant I wasn't available to my family, even when it was important to them. And this only increased as time went by.

One particular side effect of Mom living with us was that we became very tied to our home. We never traveled far and only took short vacations. In the initial years of her living with us, she sometimes went with us, but she wasn't much for road trips as time went by. At one point, we bought a cabin a few hours' drive away and vacationed there for school breaks, winter holidays, and summers, for years. We'd typically go for a long weekend. It was as good a solution as we could find. Close enough to feel we could be home quickly, when necessary, but still a great family getaway in the forest.

Mom never said anything negative about these weekends away, and later offered numerous times to be "checked in" to the local nursing home so that we could get away for a lengthier vacation. I didn't want to do that, as mentioned. So as time went by, we left her less and less, or we asked relatives to stay with her.

If Mom hadn't been such an easy person to get along with, I can see how the relationship with my husband could have been affected. I know from talking to other caregivers that there can sometimes be challenges with a spouse—including jealousy, irritation, and everything in between—when an elderly parent moves in. My husband and Mom got along really well, however. They were both very respectful of the other, and John (and our boys) doted on her. Note: the caregiving situation is defined by the state of health—and personal qualities—of the loved one, as well as the family members involved in the care.

Other caregivers don't have it so easy. There can be many family challenges, including loved ones who may feel bitter about their situation. There is often an issue of family members not pitching in to help with a loved one's care.

One caregiver, Marilyn, welcomed her husband's parents into their home and lovingly took care of them for years. Even though she was honored to do so, she also experienced the "unfairness" of his siblings being absent from the parents' care team.

When her family initially took in her in-laws, she hoped her husband's siblings might at least help out by extending invitations to the parents to come visit their homes, providing respite and some breathing room to her family—or perhaps take the parents with them on vacations, etc. But she found that they always had other plans. The siblings also expressed a different philosophy about eldercare. They believed their elderly parents were simply better off among people their own age, in a place with medical care, and that even a nursing home with the occasional visit from them and the grandkids would be enough.

Unfortunately, both "unequal caregiving" and differing caregiver philosophies among siblings is very common. Such behavior within the family can result in bad feelings, jealousy, or even anger. The fact that one sibling gets saddled with all the responsibility (never going on an extended vacation, for example), while others have their freedom and flexibility, can take its toll over time.

Martin's caregiving scenario is another example. His wife stepped in to help care for his aging father after his mother died. After many years, weekly grocery shopping morphed into a much bigger responsibility, including changing diapers and tending to personal care needs. Caregiving became a huge strain on Martin's livelihood, both due to the caregiving expenses and the loss of his own income, as he was self-employed. When he asked his siblings for help, no one answered his call. Later, when his dad's health worsened, he repeated his plea for both his siblings' time and financial support. But they always found excuses. Their lack of assistance created even more stress on Martin's mental health and finances.

As his dad had recently entered hospice, I wondered if the family would be able to come together and heal given the stressful dynamics. Listening to Martin's story, it seemed to me that he should be repaid in some way after his father passes, to compensate for his caregiving expenses and the losses to his income while caregiving.

Caregiving compensation can be a sensitive subject in many families; it is tricky to accurately calibrate the value of what a given caregiver may be doing. However, such questions are typical in family caregiving scenarios. Finances in general can be a topic of controversy and concern for both the caregiver and their extended family.

Truth #7: Money matters

Caregiving can be expensive.

Most "informal" caregivers (someone caring for a family member, spouse, or a friend, who isn't a professional caregiver or nurse) don't get paid, and a care receiver may or may not be able to afford their own medical and living expenses.

As I mentioned, I cut my hours in half, then ended up leaving the corporate world to do part-time freelancing from home. Before cutting my hours, there were some uncomfortable discussions with my management over my recurring need for time off and a reduction in travel. When I finally left my job to freelance, there was a definite drop in my income.

But there were many positive benefits to being at home. Sure, helping Mom was a major one, but it also allowed me to focus more on my children as well. I got further involved in their school activities, Boy Scouts, and other aspects of their lives. The part-time work, without the commute, was also quite wonderful. I felt very lucky.

Many of the people I interviewed were not as fortunate—they were not given the flexibility to reduce their hours or office commute to better accommodate their caregiving role. One was overlooked for promotions; another was taken off a prestigious account due to their request not to travel internationally. Keep in mind, this was decades ago and few full-time employees were allowed to work from home. Punching the clock was much more prevalent. There are countless examples of caregivers being penalized in their careers. Dementia-related caregiving has even more effect on the caregiver's ability to do other work and their need for flexibility.

Studies confirm that there can be significant effects to a caregiver's job-related income, employment longevity, and overall career opportunities.[12] Some 61 percent of caregivers are affected at their job, due to factors such as taking time off, reducing work hours, taking a leave of absence, and turning down promotions. One in five caregivers report high financial strain due to their caregiving requirements.[13] Reduction of hours can also result in the loss of health insurance and other benefits, so there can be further effects than a simple reduction in wages.

One study found that caregivers who care for an elderly adult with three or more mobility or self-care needs spend an average of 253 hours per month in their caring role. That's equivalent to almost two full-time jobs folks, without any pay.[14]

It's so wrong. Family caregivers are frequently not valued from the perspective of many employers, the government, and much of society, although that is thankfully changing. More and more companies now have eldercare and caregiving benefits: leave of absences, supportive programs for the caregiver/employee as well as the care receiver, etc. With the emergence of our post-pandemic world, the typical employment work schedule has dramatically changed for many employees, providing increased flexibility and many alternatives to being in the office.

When the family decision of "who should become caregiver?" is discussed, which hopefully it will be, all of these career and financial concerns should be considered.

Additionally, the financial situation of the loved one should be understood, as it can play an important role in how a caregiving journey unfolds. We were fortunate that my mom was financially secure to live out the remainder of her life, paying her own way. I know she'd have felt terrible if she couldn't pay her bills. So, kudos to my father for working so hard all of his life to ensure his sweet little Dee (my mom's nickname) would always be cared for.

From the moment she moved in with us, Mom painstakingly documented everything I spent on her needs (mainly prescriptions and comfort items), and she then "settled" with me every month. It was important to her. After many years of living with us, she also insisted on paying a small rent. She would laugh and say, "For the room, meals, and wonderful maid service." She was already sending the occasional check to my brother to help him out from time to time, so I didn't mind if she wrote a few to us. I thought it was sweet that she wanted to be "Even Steven."

When both of my parents were alive, I never really thought about their financial status. We weren't wealthy by any means, but we certainly weren't poor. My dad worked a lot of overtime, and we always had what we needed growing up, even if some of it was secondhand.

Dad took care of all the finances and paperwork. He put Mom on a grocery and household expense budget, practically unheard of in my generation. My parents were very frugal. I remember clipping coupons with Mom and saving up grocery store stamps. We did a lot of our clothing shopping at church and neighborhood rummage sales. If someone had asked me about my parents' financial status back then, I might have said they were just getting by, with the help of all of that overtime.

When my dad's health started to decline, and he was in and out of the hospital, I began helping my parents with the piles of medical insurance paperwork. But Dad still handled the bills. Mom was never involved in any of the finances, so she didn't know what their monthly expenses were, or what assets or income they had. One day, she expressed concern over what they could afford for my father's care. If my dad's health continued to worsen, as predicted by his doctor, she wanted him to have the option of in-home care. She didn't want to ask Dad directly, as she felt it might signal to him that he wasn't going to get better. She asked me to look at their finances. I assured her that they had Dad's pension and their social security, and also had their house to sell, if necessary. But she had planted a seed of concern, so I said I'd look into it.

Prior to his retirement, my dad was a jet mechanic working for TWA airlines. As a blue-collar worker back then, he didn't make a great deal of money—probably why he worked a lot of overtime. On top of the long hours, his commute to and from the airport was over an hour each way. He'd come home at odd hours and needed his grease-covered overalls washed almost every day. I don't recall him ever complaining about the long hours, either.

My dad on the job at San Francisco Airport

My parents bought our family home when I was a toddler. I'm sure the mortgage and other expenses were a big stretch for them at the time. They dutifully paid off their mortgage on his single income prior to his retirement. That was a huge achievement, but we'd learn Dad accomplished much more.

When I started to review their financial state, it was like trying to fit the pieces of a puzzle together. I started digging into files and boxes of records. Dad was in the hospital at the time, so it was my only chance to do this sleuthing. Amazingly, I found a file full of savings bonds Dad bought routinely out of every paycheck. My mom was shocked when I told her, and sad. They scrimped so much and put off things like vacations. At the time, she thought they didn't have the extra money, while he wanted to be secure, I guess. They would have enjoyed a beautiful, long retirement together had he lived; so, more congrats to my dad for managing to save up such a nest egg.

Based on their finances, Mom didn't have to worry about the costs for Dad's care, and they initially tried a variety of in-home care scenarios. Even when he finally needed to go to a nursing home, they had the money to pay for all the services he needed. When my father passed away, he left his little Dee with adequate funds to last her lifetime. Years later, I remember Mom was a little sticker shocked at the rent for her first apartment (after she sold the family home). I kept reassuring her she was still in good shape to cover her bills, including her prescription costs, which often surpassed $500 a month.

Note to future caregivers: finances are something you want to get an early grip on, along with whether your loved one has a will or trust, which thankfully my parents did. I could write a

62

whole book on going through that process (creating a will and/or trust, Power of Attorney, etc.), but suffice it to say, it is vital to have this early in the caregiving journey, especially if dementia is involved.

To me, the need to know the finances of your loved one is an issue of optimizing their care and comfort while they are still here, not optimizing the money they leave in their estate. However, in talking to some caregivers and their siblings, I heard many stories of family members who may have been overly focused on future inheritances. One daughter didn't take care of repairs to the family home, which could have resulted in greater comfort and safety for her elderly mom. Another kept her father at home—despite advanced dementia that was probably making it unsafe to have him there—to save on the expenses of an Alzheimer's care facility. Her dad had adequate funds that could have easily covered those expenses, but that would have reduced any future inheritances.

In my interviews, I learned that caregivers are indeed only human, and that not every action is that of a saint. And sadly, I also heard many instances where the loved one's other non-caregiver family members were also not outfitted with angel wings.

Had it been an issue for my mom, we would have gladly covered her bills. Having said that, it was nice we didn't have to. I'm sure it made her feel better to pay her own way, as it was important to her that she maintain some level of independence, as well as not be a burden.

I feel for people where caregiving finances become a source of stress or ill-will within the family. Sometimes the financial ramifications of various caregiving decisions create deep divides within families that last long after their loved one passes.

Kathleen is one example of how finances can strain family dynamics. Her elderly mom moved in with her, and she did not ask for any rent or financial contribution from her mom nor her extended family. Kathleen paid for visiting care and other caregiving expenses. Her siblings never offered assistance of any kind, financial or otherwise. They did express concerns, however, over equity in the inheritance. Their focus on the will rather than their mother's care created a rift in the family, with the sole caregiver at odds with the rest of the siblings. I've heard variations of this from others, unfortunately.

Sometimes a parent may choose to leave a greater inheritance to the caregiving child, which can result in a huge divide among siblings. Should the caregiver sibling get paid while caring for a loved one? Should that sibling get a greater inheritance? Some people agree that an adult son or daughter providing care for a parent should receive a larger inheritance, others do not.[15] It is not uncommon for an executor of a trust to be compensated for their role, so it could certainly be argued that the even greater role of caregiver should possibly receive compensation.

I personally think this determination is unique to each given caregiving situation. As mentioned earlier, Martin took on a large financial burden when he and his wife cared for his father. He paid all his dad's caregiving expenses, and caring for his dad impacted the income from his own business as well. In his case, I feel he should be compensated in some way.

Having said that, I also don't think caregiving alone *entitles* people to more of an inheritance. It all depends. What is the caregiver sacrificing (career, family, finances, etc.), and whose money is being used to provide the care? Could others in the family even help given their own unique situation? This is a challenging question, as a person's inability to help is often not something they can easily change. The problem may be the location or size of their home or financial constraints. What is the extent of care involved? Dropping in one day a week, with professional in-home caregivers doing all the work, is different from moving a parent into your home and providing full-time care. One sibling may take care of a parent for a while, and then another sibling may take the reins later on.

While I use the term "sacrificing," we must also not forget the incredible blessings that caregiving most often brings. I was the logical choice to care for my mom (location, job flexibility, husband's medical insurance, etc.). But I also *wanted* to be her caregiver (likely due to the family script passed down to me by caring parents). I felt very fortunate that Mom could live with us. Plus, she had the means to avoid being a financial burden.

Years before she passed, Mom wanted to update her will and leave the bulk of her money to me, since she was living in our home and my family was caring for her. She and my father had earlier helped my brother purchase a house and helped with a few other financial matters, so she thought this change would be equitable. But I thought it was too much, and I didn't feel like we needed to be "rewarded" for her care. Plus, she paid for her medical expenses and more. I encouraged her to leave equal inheritances to my brother and me, which she reluctantly did.

I know, however, that oftentimes such equity doesn't occur. I heard one instance of a daughter who was absent from her mom's life for decades, only to re-engage with her elderly mom and promptly focus on subtle hints that she needed the future inheritance more than her siblings. She started taking her mom to medical appointments, and before her appreciative siblings realized what was going on, their mom made that daughter her sole beneficiary. The other siblings never talked to their sister after their mom's passing.

Every situation is unique. I think this is why it is important for families to talk about the topic of finances before it becomes an issue. I would also encourage families to continue to dialogue about financial matters, as the situation (for all family members) can and does change over time.

As I look around at my many "Boomer-aged" friends (most are either retired or approaching retirement) who are still caregiving for a parent, I'm struck at how important this finance topic can be, especially as the caregivers themselves are aging.

My mother was an older mom, and I was only in my early fifties when she passed away at ninety-three. Today, I see that a number of my friends in their mid to late sixties are having to make caregiving decisions, perhaps still trying to get their eighty-plus-year-old parent to move out of the family home, while also managing their own retirement planning. At least one is faced with helping to finance their parent's remaining years as they enter a time when they themselves will be on a fixed income.

Finances should be discussed and understood, and experts agree that families should consider creating a personal caregiver agreement if either real-time compensation or a greater inheritance will be provided for the sibling providing care.

Also, as mentioned earlier, being a caregiver does not make someone a saint. There is the opportunity for undue influence to occur with a caregiver isolating a loved one from others, making the care receiver dependent on them, influencing changes in the will, etc. As my dad always said, "Paper never forgets." Write things down early in the process. Ensuring a loved one fully documents their wishes—and having the appropriate legal documents, including a will and trust—can help keep a family from imploding.

Truth #8: You'll likely need a lifeline (ask for two)

Every corpse on Mt. Everest was once an extremely motivated person.
Unknown

I spoke earlier of the importance of having family and friends as an initial line of caregiving support. A lot of caregivers wait too long to ask for and leverage that assistance. Many also shy away from pulling in other resources and professional help until fairly late in their caregiving. I like this Mt. Everest quote, as it's a great *visual* reminder of why caregivers need to ask for help and not do it all alone.

Mt. Everest is an all-encompassing task, and you have to be motivated and dedicated to prepare for it, embark on it, sustain your climb, stay healthy, and remain able to physically and mentally endure the entire process from start to finish. Even with the best planning, there can be many obstacles, both expected and unexpected. A climber can stumble and not be able to continue, but they can also move forward knowing that they did something beyond what they ever thought possible.

Caregiving is like that.

You are fully motivated to dedicate your energy, time, and emotions to a loved one. You willingly and lovingly embark on the caregiving journey with great passion and enthusiasm. If you are caring for a parent, there is satisfaction in helping the one person who probably has most helped you in life, made sacrifices for you, and loves you. If you are caring for a spouse, it is someone you love who is central to your life, and likely your family's life, too.

You begin that climb, and at some point, you may start to become exhausted. You also ultimately may realize you are climbing to an inevitable finish line you can't change. That may be the toughest part of all.

In climbing, while abilities and focus are paramount, nature can throw obstacles at you that can defeat you—a sudden and treacherous storm, for example. In caregiving, there can be myriad obstacles that present themselves. Your loved one's health may worsen, your own health may become problematic, a lack of adequate finances may create difficulties, or your own life circumstances may suddenly shift (getting a divorce, losing a job, etc.).

How the climber or the caregiver is able to adapt to these obstacles, can make or break them.

A climber may slip but be saved by a tether to another climber. Roped climbing provides a lifeline should an unexpected obstacle present itself, or should one realize they have overestimated their abilities for their journey's challenges. A solo climber, on the other hand, does not have this type of safety net.

Such is the case of a caregiver. Going solo and doing it all yourself may result in you falling off track or becoming overwhelmed in some way—negatively affecting your own health or potentially even that of your loved one. I'm not inferring you will die (literally becoming a corpse) if you try and do it all alone, but I am emphasizing that the potential mental and physical effects of not having support can be significant. They shouldn't be underestimated or ignored. Yet, so many of the caregivers I spoke with did much of their caregiving solo, at least, until far into their journey (frequently until a loved one entered hospice).

My mom overtaxed herself and risked her health in order to keep my ailing father in the comfort and familiarity of his home. She wouldn't listen to what the doctors told her; she wasn't based in the reality of Dad's deteriorating health. She kept climbing up that very steep mountain for a very long time. Yes, I helped when I could, but there were so many other lifelines she could have reached out to but didn't.

His illness lasted some five or six years. The specific diagnosis isn't important, but its onset was sudden and quite unexpected. He had some emergency surgery and recovered from the actual procedure, but he never regained his previous good health. He lost a lot of weight and became considerably less energetic. He was in and out of the hospital after that, and his condition only worsened.

He started having a lot of trouble getting around. One day, when he was still living at home, Mom called and said he tripped and fell to the floor. She asked if I could come help her get him back into bed. I asked if she needed an ambulance. She responded adamantly that he didn't want to be taken to the hospital, only lifted from the floor. She seemed frantic, so I dropped what I was doing and drove the thirty minutes to their home. When I got there, he was flat on the floor, clearly in pain. I wanted to call 911, but he refused. First, he commanded, then begged.

So instead, I called a male family friend who came to help. Now keep in mind, my dad was at least 6'2", and even though he had lost weight, he was still heavier than many people might be able to lift, even with help. The two of us lifted my dad and placed him on his bed. A more appropriate description might be that we threw him on his bed. It was not a gentle movement because of his size. He screamed in agony, and I thought for sure we hurt him. I don't know if it was the original fall or moving him onto the bed that caused his injuries. It was probably a combination of both.

When I wouldn't leave, he said he was fine. I didn't believe him, but couldn't think of another option at that moment. When I left, he was no longer groaning in pain, and my mom was already in the kitchen fixing him something to eat. I reluctantly went home.

The next day, Mom desperately called me back to the house to check on him. When I saw him again, I decided something needed to be done. He was conscious and not complaining, but looked in distress. He said he was fine, but he seemed pale and clammy. I decided the reason he wasn't complaining was to conceal his pain so he didn't have to be taken to the hospital. He had a fever and looked ill, so finally, against his wishes, I called 911. They came, and it took three firefighters to carry him away on a stretcher. He screamed in pain when they moved him. I was in tears. It was so hard to see him like that.

Dad broke several bones, and we didn't realize it because of his efforts to hide the pain. His doctor predicted more falls due to his weakened state and worsening health. After a great deal of argument, my dad agreed to be discharged from the hospital to recuperate in a nursing home. It was temporary to get his strength back so he could walk. I don't remember how long he was there for, but do recall how much he hated the place. Thankfully, he regained some strength and eventually went home.

Over time, however, his use of a walker was even a struggle, and he became pretty much bedridden. Mom tried several care scenarios in the home, but nothing worked. There would be many more 911 calls, injuries, and more than a few ousted care providers. She finally told him that he needed to return to the nursing home until his health and mobility improved. I am not sure if she believed it was a temporary solution or was trying to put a positive face on a dismal transition, but it was the necessary and right thing for her to do. Keeping him at home could have resulted in continued accidents, ambulance trips, and indignities. I had seen him flat on the floor screaming in pain more than once—downright heart-wrenching.

I was also worried about my mom's health at the time. Even with in-home care assistance, Dad wanted Mom to be his primary caregiver and do most everything, with the care provider often standing in the wings doing nothing. It wasn't long before the toll on her physical and mental health could be seen. It was dizzying to watch her. I thought more than once that caregiving was the toughest job in the world. As a new mom, my days often felt overwhelming caring for a tiny baby. But here, as I watched all that my mom was doing each day, I was amazed at her mental and physical fortitude.

When she eventually decided he needed to be in a nursing home, Mom finally embraced the important truth that caregiving for my dad—loving him and making him as comfortable as possible—didn't mean she did all of the work herself. She finally reached for a lifeline. But, boy, did she feel guilty about that.

Truth #9: You're doing the best you can (so stop feeling guilty)

So why don't caregivers tether themselves to needed help and resources? Why don't they accept their limitations and recognize there are points on that mountain when they truly might fall? Why don't they ask for a lifeline, or two, or three?

Why do caregivers do all they can do—often *exceed* what they physically and mentally should do; and then feel they need to do even more? And then, why do they feel so guilty?

Guilt that we're not doing enough for our loved one, or that we're somehow not being the superhuman our family needs while we're focusing on caregiving. Guilt over not being able to do everything ourselves, or guilt over our inability to provide certain care. Some feel selfish when they prioritize self-care.

Common is the guilt experienced over being short with a loved one. Many caregivers experience impatience over a behavior that is inherent in the care receiver's disease or a particular medication they may be taking. For example, medications might make a loved one sleepy, more prone to needing to urinate, or even more hungry. Dementia, of course, comes with a whole set of behaviors that can cause negative reactions in others and the caregiver, but are not within the control of the person with dementia.

Then there's guilt over caregiving decisions; and possibly guilt over disagreements with other family members about those decisions. The list goes on and on. There is even survivor's guilt when a loved one dies.

Caregiver guilt is inevitable. You need to realize that and cut yourself some slack. You're doing the best you can—most likely accomplishing more than you ever thought you could, and probably doing things beyond what you should.

My mother felt enormous guilt after she moved Dad into a nursing home, even though she continued to be his primary caregiver in many ways. Every day, Mom went to the nursing home, where she sat with him. She brought the mail and her lunch. He'd review the bills and advise her on any paperwork or issue at the house. She talked with him about whatever she could that was positive and happy. But they often ended up talking about his terrible situation, how unfair life was, and how much he hated the nursing home and wanted to go home. That was sheer misery for both of them, I'm sure.

Although he had 24-hour care at the nursing home, Mom was always there, and still his primary caregiver. She provided comfort, love, and support as best she could, and spared no expense in the energies and emotions she devoted to that care. She stayed with him all day and tended to his needs, even though it was physically difficult as she was so tiny. To turn him or help him sit up was almost impossible. And I know it was mentally exhausting as well.

She tried to get the staff to be more respectful of him, so he could retain some level of dignity and privacy. Given he was bedridden, this was difficult and tricky. Dad described the staff as "hellish," but I truly believed they were doing the best that they could in a bleak and challenging situation. He hated it there and he let them know it, often. Understandably, my father was angry—he felt cheated and disappointed by his fate. He was also upset by how his deterioration had affected my mother and their future life together.

The nursing home was only a few miles away from my parents' house. It was in a nice area and rated well, and Dad's doctor was on-call there. It seemed like a good choice. But it was still a nursing home and a dreary place. Many of the people living there were not ambulatory. Some were not able to communicate. For a while, my dad was rooming with a man who constantly moaned in pain. We ended up moving him into his own room after that.

Mom did what she could to make Dad more comfortable. She tried to bring light into his very dark world. She tried to figure out a way for him to come home. She just kept climbing that mountain and refused to look down.

There were some happy moments from time to time. Sometimes my mom arranged for Dad to return to their home for the day. I visited at those times. She hired an aide to help transfer my dad into a wheelchair and navigate steps into the home. Getting him to the toilet was a challenge due to narrow bathrooms that were difficult to access with the wheelchair. But we made it work as best we could. He relished those days. Home was such a comfortable place for him, and he yearned to be back there permanently.

After one such trip and seeing how happy Dad was at home, Mom tried once again to move him back home, against his doctor's recommendation. It didn't work for a number of reasons, the primary one being the physical requirements it meant for Mom. My dad couldn't deal with strangers in the house overnight, so he wouldn't agree to round-the-clock care. Having no physical assistance overnight proved problematic and then, finally, impossible. Additionally, his health continued to deteriorate at a quickened pace. It was only a few days into the new arrangement when Mom had the difficult talk about him returning to the nursing home. That was hard for both of them, as it was the first time they were on the same page about the permanency of his situation. They both realized he could no longer live at home. And in fact, he wasn't going to get any better.

My mom felt great sadness over this permanency. She talked about how she had let him down. She felt enormous guilt. I knew she hadn't let my dad down, but nothing I said helped. She also thought Dad's out-of-state family felt critical of the nursing home decision. I told her they were simply sad and shocked, as he was always so healthy and vibrant.

At the time, Dad's brother asked a lot of questions about the nursing home decision, wondering if there were any other options. He visited once when my father was already permanently in the nursing home. He was quite shocked to see first-hand his brother's declining health condition. I don't know what conversations he and Dad, or he and Mom, had back then. I just know she felt like she was somehow the bad guy.

Frankly, I wasn't sure what my uncle or other distant relatives thought, but I told my mom they hadn't lived the situation, so how could they understand? Looking back and thinking about what I now know about caregiver's guilt, I'm sure that none of the relatives thought anything negative about Mom, only sad about my father's situation. I appreciated that after Dad's death, his brother (love you Uncle Joe) reached out to my mom in a letter, in an attempt to validate her decisions and release her from this guilt. I'm not sure, though, if it ever really did.

I experienced caregiver guilt, too. I never felt like I did enough for my father. I remember going to visit him while I was pregnant, and then later with my infant—and then toddler—son. The visits were often difficult, as Dad was miserable and sometimes quite emotional about his terrible circumstances. Since he was bedridden, many of the visits ended up with my son crawling around on the hospital bed or even on the floor. By that point, it was quite difficult to get my father into a wheelchair to move him out to the garden or a common area within the nursing home. There wasn't much we could do beyond simply hanging out in my dad's dreary room. Even so, I always felt Dad enjoyed his grandson's visits. He'd give him bear hugs on his chest and would smile, one of the few times he did in those days. We never stayed long, though, as it always seemed to be stressful given the nursing home environment and my dad's medical requirements.

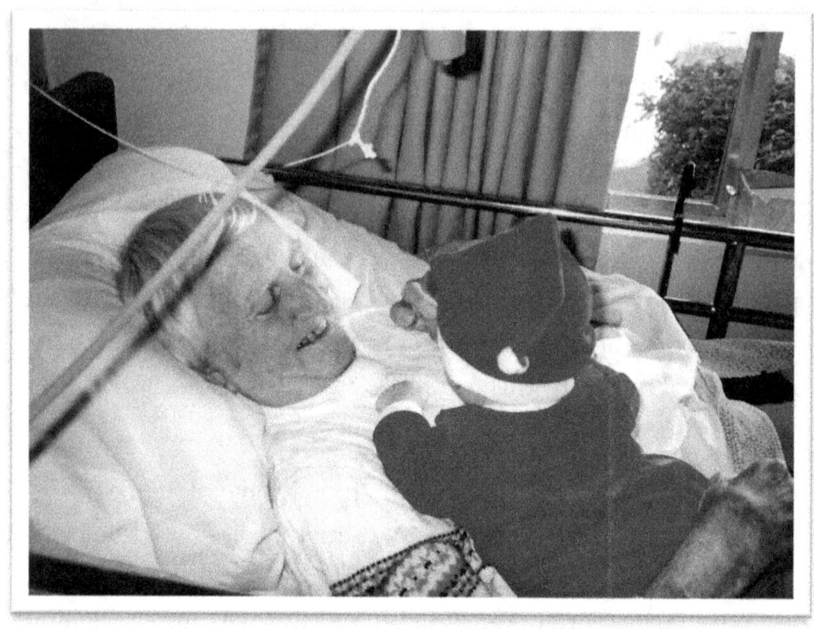

Christmas hugs with Grampa at the nursing home

I wish some of those final memories with my father were happier ones, but all I can remember was being sad and stressed about my not being able to improve his situation, and feeling guilty about not spending more time with him. I often felt like I was shortchanging everyone in my life whom I loved: Dad, my husband, my sons, and my friends. The feelings of guilt and regret only increased after he died.

Later, while caring for my mom, guilt would crop up over the smallest thing. When Mom first moved in with us, she would wash any dirty dishes left in the sink. Sometimes she left food on the dishes because she couldn't see well. For a while I simply re-washed them, but after coming across a particularly nasty dirty plate in the cupboard one day, I finally told her to stop doing the dishes as she wasn't getting them clean. I'm fairly certain I came across as negative and snappish. She was visibly heartbroken. I didn't think about how useless it might make her feel. Oh, did I feel like crap later. *Guilty as charged!*

A few times, friends came over for dinner, and I'd ask Mom to sit at the kitchen table with our kids while I, my husband and our friends sat in the dining room. It wasn't meant as a slight to her, but an opportunity for us to enjoy our friends as a "normal" couple, versus our typical family of five. But it wouldn't have been hard to have included her at the dinner table with "the adults." I sometimes felt guilty about excluding her.

I still vividly recall an event with Mom when I lost my temper and yelled at her—loudly—for several minutes. She had befriended a couple she had met at the community center. They were my age, and suddenly this couple inserted themselves into Mom's personal life. They started calling her frequently, and then they came out to our house for a visit. They asked too many personal questions and seemed to already know way too much about her. Their interest in her seemed odd. I told Mom I thought they were pushy people and that I didn't understand the connection. I told her to be cautious and not to give them any more personal information. But she dismissed them as "nice people who were simply trying to be friendly."

Then one day while doing her bills, I found she'd written a $1000 check to them the day before. They apparently asked her for a loan. I confronted her, and my loud voice escalated into a yell. I remember actually kicking over a piece of furniture as I lost my temper. I yelled for several minutes. I was mad that she was "taken" by this couple, even after I warned her. I made my poor sweet mom cry that day.

Thankfully, we were able to cancel the check. I later called the couple and left a less-than-friendly message on their telephone answering machine, stating that if they contacted my mom again, I'd call the police. We never heard from them after that. While I suppose my anger and irritation were directed at them and not Mom, she suffered the brunt of it, and it was a long time before I stopped feeling guilty about losing my temper with her.

Even now, over a decade after my mom's death, I occasionally have a memory of some small thing that I ought to have done differently. It's been three decades since my father's death, and I still feel guilty that I didn't do more. I still cringe at the thought of his final days. Guilt is relentless.

One person that I interviewed, Mandy, shared that she would take her husband to the movies when he was in an early stage of Alzheimer's. He loved movies, and the two frequented them often. They sat in the same exact location, near the back and near the doors leading to the men's bathroom. He always did fine at getting back and forth to the bathroom.

On one particular movie date, at some point towards the end of the movie, Mandy's husband needed to go to the bathroom. He got up and left. Time went by… the movie was almost done. Mandy knew he wasn't back, but thought he always did okay previously, and besides, she wanted to see the last few minutes of the movie. When the movie ended later, she went and looked for her husband. She asked another theater patron if her husband was in the bathroom. He wasn't there. As Mandy headed towards the entrance, there was her spouse being escorted by a theater worker. Her husband couldn't remember how to get back to their seats. He was extremely agitated and was crying.

Mandy said she felt ashamed for watching the end of the movie while her husband was missing. The guilt was so strong—and her fear of it happening again so great—that they never went back to the movies.

Theresa was determined to keep her aging mom out of a nursing home, so she invited her mom to move in with her. Rental income from her mom's home initially covered her medical costs. But as her mom's health deteriorated, Theresa decided to hire in-home care. Her siblings expressed concerns over the added costs (and dwindling inheritance) while offering no assistance to Theresa. Even though it was her mom's money, Theresa felt she was being selfish by bringing in professional care. At the same time, she resented the attitude of her siblings. When she finally confronted her siblings over their greed and lack of help, she felt tremendous guilt over the resultant deteriorating relationships. *Caregiver guilt, anyone?*

It was only many years after Mom's passing that I finally acknowledged that my caregiver guilt—and probably most caregiver guilt—was unwarranted and self-imposed. I finally recognized that the bulk of it came from deep within, an unnerving forensic analysis that many caregivers put themselves through. What could have been handled better?

What didn't I do right? How could I have done that? How could I *not* have done that?

Most caregivers don't cut themselves enough slack. Maybe they don't have the time to do so. So much about caregiving—especially in the later stages of caring for a loved one—is a reaction. There isn't time for a lot of thought, planning, or deliberation concerning what is the best decision. You react. You simply do. You make decisions with the information you have. When you do plan, the plan is often interrupted. You hope, you pray, and later, you second-guess yourself.

The nagging doubt creeps in, followed by the guilt. This is often the plight of a caregiver, and the question always being asked is, "What if I had done something differently?"

Chapter 7

Why am I so hot, moody, and tired?

Along with many caregivers being sandwiched between parenting their young kids and caring for their elderly parents, guess what? Many female caregivers are going through "the change" at the same time.

If you are a male reading this and have a female in your life going through menopause while caregiving, take note: she will need extra love and self-care. She may be mourning the loss of her younger self while also losing a loved one, and her caregiving stress may be significantly intensifying menopause-related symptoms.

Mom moved in when I was forty-three, after I cared for her remotely for many years. Although the average age for menopause is fifty-one, I was one of the approximately 5 percent of women who experience "early" menopause in their early forties.[16]

So along with parenting two young and rambunctious boys, working, caregiving, and handling all of the typical household things that most people do, my body and mind started to turn on me at the same time my mom moved in. I had difficulty sleeping, which resulted in incredible fatigue and a Starbucks drive-thru coffee addiction, which lasted for many years. I was freezing one minute, and miserably hot the next. There were a few anxious and teary-eyed episodes at work.

I initially attributed all of this to stress and our chaotic life. I thought I was too young for menopause, even though I started to experience hot flashes. I wasn't aware of something called "early menopause" and wasn't educated on the wide variety of symptoms associated with it. Thinking back, I'm not sure if I experienced other common menopause symptoms like mood swings (my husband lovingly says that I did) and memory issues (oops, I can't recall). I only remember suffering with the hot flashes, anxiety, and lack of sleep.

I finally raised my symptoms to my OB/GYN at an annual checkup. The early menopause diagnosis was confirmed based on the symptoms and end of my period. I wasn't tested for hormone imbalances or deficiencies, but I did ask my doctor about hormone replacement therapy. At the time, she expressed some concerns over my undergoing estrogen therapy, as her view was that I had minimal symptoms to manage. She said to try some herbs for the hot flashes, and that they should eventually improve over time.

But they didn't, at least not for some time. Sadly, I didn't know back then that natural hormone therapies and other interventions—such as supplements and dietary/lifestyle modifications—could have helped reduce my symptoms and improve my daily life. I don't think hormone imbalances were something women talked about a lot with their doctors or friends at that time (at least I didn't). But thankfully, I feel that has changed over the past several decades, and I've met many middle-aged women now who are taking bio-identical hormones (including estrogen, progesterone, and DHEA) to greatly reduce their menopause-related symptoms.

Know that the hormone imbalances that occur with menopause, as well as leading up to and after menopause, can be overwhelming. A woman can become anxious and feel like she is on an emotional rollercoaster. Menopause symptoms usually don't improve for some time, and in many cases, may get worse. Ignoring symptoms or trying to wait patiently for them to pass are not helpful strategies.

Hormone imbalances can also make women less resilient, so all of the physical and mental stressors that come with caregiving can have a magnified effect on our health. Our immunity, as well as our ability to cope, can be affected. Both of these are of particular concern to caregivers needing to be available and attentive to loved ones.

Our mental health can also be impacted. In fact, studies have shown that middle-aged and older women who provide care for an ill spouse are almost six times more likely to suffer anxious or depressive symptoms as women with no caregiving responsibilities.[17]

If you find that you (or a female caregiver in your life) are suffering after your mid-thirties (when a woman's hormones start to go crazy as she begins the transition to menopause), know that a lot of wonderful resources are available to help.

I recommend you visit this link on Dr. Cabeca's website (https://drannacabeca.com/pages/breeze-through-menopause). There are many educational articles and podcasts available on her site as well.

Caregiving and other sources of stress can worsen symptoms and one's overall menopause experience. Fatigue, insomnia, anxiety, depression, weight gain, and many additional symptoms can be experienced or exacerbated.

Research has found that caregiving—especially as a sandwich generation caregiver—significantly increases the odds of a woman having more intense psychological and physical symptoms during menopause compared to non-caregivers.[18] Yet another reason caregivers need to implement strategies to reduce—*or at least better manage*—their stress.

Chapter 8

Physical and mental stress

It's not the load that breaks you down. It's the way you carry it.
Lena Horne

There are a lot of baby boomers who have cared for or who are currently caring for their aging parents. Approximately 80 percent of boomers surveyed in one group study reported experiencing strains in their relationships during their caregiving years. About 25 percent of divorced people in this group felt that caregiving played a major role in their divorce.[19] I'm not saying that your caregiving experience will result in divorce, but I do believe there are certainties about caregiving that frequently cause stress and poor coping in the majority of caregivers. Caregiving's potential for stress is real and shouldn't be dismissed.

When someone mentions they are in caregiving mode, a common response is, "Take care of yourself, as I'm sure you are under a lot of stress."

Then, a typical reply by the caregiver will usually focus on the positives of caring for a loved one—they may respond with something like, "Yes, but there are many more blessings."

That's why I always refer to caregiving as a period of "blessings and stressings." We are usually happy to be doing it, and we are most often feeling blessed to be able to help our loved ones. But if we're completely honest, we also know that caregiving comes with no shortage of stressful moments.

There are challenges in balancing parenting and work with caregiving responsibilities, including the stress of watching a loved one decline, the emotional effects of managing problematic behaviors, and the negative effects of not managing one's own health—especially chronic conditions. Trading off self-care can take its toll as well. I remind you that caregiver stress has been associated with a reduction in immune system health and increased psychological distress.

In particular, caregivers can become isolated. Friendships and other social connections can become deprioritized. Your self-identity and enjoyment of life as your true self may be displaced by the notion that you are not "you"—with all of the things that make you unique and give you pleasure—so much as you are someone else's caregiver.

When my mom was in the midst of a medical crisis, I dropped off the radar. My friends knew when something was up, as I would disappear from my usual communications. This was before I (and many of my peers) had joined Facebook, so there wasn't an easy way to update my entire community of friends and family, and also gain immediate love and support. As an aside, I joined Facebook a few months after Mom died in 2009; guess I needed some extra support and virtual hugs.

Women are more vulnerable to the effects of this type of reduced social support and connection. Fortunately, there are now many websites affiliated with organizations (like the Alzheimer's Association) that provide care or focus on particular diseases. Many of these offer a wealth of caregiving information, as well as community chatrooms where caregivers can ask questions, share best practices, and commiserate. Take advantage of them.

I think about some of the people I interviewed and can feel their sense of isolation. One woman, Mandy, is becoming more and more isolated as her husband's Alzheimer's worsens. While part of this is her need to focus on him and ensure he's not left alone, it's also true that other people often struggle to include someone in their lives who is caring for a loved one.

Additionally, friends of people with Alzheimer's often don't know how to cope with a deteriorating friend. Many of Mandy's husband's friends have disappeared. A few tried to connect early on, but as the disease advanced, it was too difficult for them to know what to say or do. The couples they knew were also at a loss in regards to how to continue the friendship. People wanted to invite Mandy to a function (say a dinner party), but didn't feel comfortable inviting her husband. Then there was the challenge of finding care coverage if she wanted to go solo. Mandy said, "I'm really too exhausted most of the time, so [I'm] not in the mood for most social activities anyway."

Frank said it's hard for many people to deal with: "Her friends used to stop by, but those visits are now very infrequent. Many of our couple friends don't really call any more—it is just too difficult or uncomfortable for many people. Nearby family tries to help by checking in, but what can people really do at this point? Earlier on, I felt guilty if I left her alone, and she didn't like it either. She is now at the point where she shouldn't be left alone, and she doesn't really tolerate other caregivers very well."

Suzanne was the caregiver for her spouse, who had advanced Parkinson's and was mostly wheelchair-bound, leaving her feeling stranded at home. Friends disappeared as his health deteriorated. She could bring in help and leave him, but participating in social events as a couple became impossible. Even family gatherings became stressful as he struggled to eat and manage daily tasks. Ultimately, she decided not to participate anymore, which caused her a good deal of guilt and stress on top of her isolation.

Alzheimer's in particular can affect the caregiving spouse and their feeling of isolation and stress. Frank says, "I love my wife, but feel so alone. First, we lost physical intimacy. When she could still talk, it was challenging, but at least we could express ourselves and connect. Now I have no conversation with anyone most days, as I am home with her much of the time."

Caregivers of people with Alzheimer's often say that they lose their loved ones twice: first, through the anguish of watching their minds diminish, their personalities fade, and their ability to communicate decline—often long before the body shuts down.

I think my husband and I became socially isolated as a couple later on in Mom's time with us when she became less able to be left alone. Luckily, many good friends checked on me and pulled me back up to the surface. We were also surrounded by a great community of couples who made an extra effort to keep us engaged with them.

There can definitely be physical stressors, too. In Mom's final year or so, when she couldn't get around well or when she was finally bedridden, there were many physical requirements that were very difficult for me—some I probably shouldn't have taken on. I think of the physical toll my dad's home care had taken on Mom. Studies have found that people caring for a spouse or parent are at a greater risk of physical strain and declining health, especially those caring for someone with Alzheimer's or dementia, and those living with the care receiver. The age of the caregiver also comes into play. Caregivers over sixty-five experience much greater physical strain.[20]

Many caregivers find their sleep is disrupted; mealtime may become "easier" with packaged (less healthy) food. If a caregiver previously had an outside passion like tennis or golf, that too can go by the wayside. Travel plans may no longer be feasible with a loved one needing attention. Self-care routines can disappear, resulting in greater stress and additional symptoms. It can become a vicious cycle and take a significant toll on a person's mental and overall health.

Frank admitted that during the past six months of his wife's Alzheimer's journey, he felt like he needed to have an alcohol intervention. He started drinking each night to dilute and manage his depressed state and stress. Frank said, "All of our lifelong dreams of future happiness (retirement travel, sharing time with grandkids, etc.) have been replaced by the depressing reality of this chronic disease."

According to one AARP report, nearly two-thirds of male caregivers indicated their caregiving was moderately to very stressful. Almost half of male caregivers were found to need time off from work. Almost half said they experienced moderate to severe physical strain while caregiving.[21]

The caregiving journey can be relentless and daunting. It can and will be stressful along the way, whether you want to acknowledge that or not (*but please do*).

You can't always get rid of caregiving stressors. Your loved one may be in decline no matter what you do. You may have significant work/caregiver scheduling conflicts, etc. But you *can* improve your stress management. One important way to do this is to accept the caregiving reality that there will be particularly difficult days. You can't let a bad day, however, result in a constant fear over what comes next. A second thing you can do is prioritize your own health and well-being. I'll talk about both of these.

Truth #10: Accept that there will be difficult days

Some days there won't be a song in your heart. Sing anyway.
Emory Austin

I love this quote, and there were a few days when I did not feel like singing, usually during a health emergency when I didn't have a solid Plan B. On those days, however, I did at least try and manage to hum.

For many people, the degree of stress, and type of stress (physical, mental, or emotional), will fluctuate depending on the health situation of their loved one as they decline or have a short-term crisis. I know mine did. When things were status quo (and I was singing), I managed everything, and don't recall feeling overly stressed or depressed.

But after a medical emergency, there was always a period of waiting for the other shoe to drop. Every time Mom experienced a heart attack or adverse health event, my anxiety level increased. There was one time in particular that rocked me to my core. It wasn't her heart that attacked her that day, it was something much more frightening.

One afternoon, Mom said she felt very ill with a strong headache and chills. It got worse, and her whole body started stiffening. Her symptoms progressed quickly and were obviously quite painful. I called 911; five firefighters and two paramedics showed up. At least one had been at our home before. By then, Mom was starting to breathe heavily, and confusion was setting in.

One paramedic believed she might have something contagious like meningitis, in part due to the rapid onset of her stiffening neck and body. They immediately transported her to the ER, where they sealed her in a plastic-covered area as they evaluated her for a contagious disease. It was incredibly scary to have her in seclusion like that. It turned out to be sepsis. We never learned the initial cause. Down came the plastic, and we finally went in to see her. Very unnerving, though. And the stress of, "What's going to happen next?" ruined my sleep for weeks. I was so anxious and afraid of that next bad thing that was undoubtedly coming.

I finally did a little self-analysis in order to better manage my stress level and get some needed sleep. The reality was that my mom usually recovered well from almost every adverse health event, and the second shoe never dropped. So having an ever-increasing level of anxiety wasn't helpful nor necessary based on my mom's medical history. I also reminded myself that we were surrounded by a good support network, with a very responsive fire department and paramedics only a few miles away.

Taking the time to think it through, I was able to get back to the reality of my mom's current situation. Things were relatively stable most of the time. The next terrible event wasn't lurking right around the corner. Sure, there'd likely be more challenging days at some point in the future, but I didn't have to live every day with anxiety and fear.

Most of the caregivers I talked to agreed that it is important to expect difficult days—but don't let them turn *every* day into something foreboding or scary. Try to focus on what's really going on, and don't overwhelm yourself by imagining only bad days ahead. Have those lifelines ready should you need them. Being as prepared as possible, and not going solo, can help when those difficult days do come along.

Truth #11: Self-care is not selfish, it's essential

You can't pour from an empty cup. Take care of yourself first.
Norm Kelly

If you don't take care of yourself, you may find you are unable to care for your loved one. Self-care is especially important for handling the difficult days in your future. It will help you better manage mental, emotional, and physical stress.

A good analogy is a rechargeable battery. If you have a flashlight and the battery is dead, it isn't much help in the storm and blackout. But if you recharge that battery, in case you need it, your light can shine through, even in the darkest hours.

Self-care can include everything from taking a relaxing bath to caring for your own health (i.e. not blowing off a yearly mammogram or medical appointment). It can be *not* canceling lunch with a best friend, or it can be *not* choosing to ignore your own unhealthy symptoms (elevated blood pressure, suspicious moles on your skin, high blood sugar readings, pain, etc.). It is well-documented that caregivers routinely deprioritize their health and don't take sufficient physical and mental respite.

In the final months that my mom was in hospice, I finally hired an aide to help with the "heavy lifting" and personal care. Kato was wonderful. This loving and gentle woman came in for a few hours a day to bathe Mom and help with her personal needs. The idea was that I'd use this time for rest or self-care. Most of the time, I would go into the garden and simply breathe. It always recharged me, at least for a time.

But it likely wasn't enough. I wish I'd spent more time using this respite to reconnect with my family. I believe an important aspect of self-care is focusing on the well-being and care of your immediate family *beyond* your care receiver. As Mom's health worsened and her need for my focus increased, I definitely de-prioritized my sons' and husband's needs. Oh, I'm fairly sure they understood and didn't take it personally, but they were hurting, too, witnessing Mom's deterioration and later realizing that hospice meant our little Granny wasn't long for this world. I wasn't really "available" to help them through that.

I still feel bad about not being more tuned in to my kids' feelings at the time. The day Mom could no longer walk, she asked to talk with her grandsons. I brought them in, one at a time. They sat on the bed, and she spoke with them in her thoughtful way. "Be kind to your mom. Be a good boy. Don't take drugs." A list was recited to each boy, and I'm fairly sure they promised to follow her instructions to the letter. They each gave her a hug and a kiss. They were extremely upset, and I tried to comfort them. But when their Granny later went into a week-long coma, I became hyper-focused on her, and did not think to spend more time and energy helping my sons cope. It was a difficult time for them, I know.

I previously mentioned buying a cabin so we could take our vacations nearby. The two-and-a-half-hour drive was intentional: be close enough to get home quickly, but be able to get away from home for some stress reduction. Conflicting goals, when you think about it. We'd rent our cabin when we weren't using it, and that was often stressful in its own way. But having it for our family was our only getaway opportunity at that time.

While my kids loved our cabin, they sometimes asked why we didn't go to Hawaii or someplace cool for our vacations, like their friends did, or why we couldn't be away from home longer than our typical long weekend. In retrospect, we probably should have. Early on, my mom could have been fine on her own for a week, and I could have asked a friend or neighbor to stop in and/or "be on call." Mom had even suggested it multiple times. But for some reason, we limited our away time. That caregiver guilt thing again? It seemed out of the question to go that far away, in particular someplace requiring air travel. This was especially so in the final few years when Mom's physical health eroded—leaving her was more stressful than not going on a vacation. Looking back, though, it would have been a healthy thing for the four of us, and I think my mom would have been fine with some type of temporary care.

Some caregivers, however, say not to focus on oneself; there will be time to do that later. Katie is one. She still carries incredible guilt from memories where she prioritized herself, her marriage, her career, or her own interests over the care of her aging mom.

Katie said, "People need to buck up. Spend as much time as you can with your loved one. You will never get that time back. Do not think anything else is more important – not work, not shopping, not helping others. Do not let one day go by without holding your loved one's hand and telling her how much you love her. When people tell you that you need to take time for yourself, remember you will have lots of time for yourself when your loved one is gone. Every single second you lose with her will never be replaced."

I didn't focus a lot on self-care. I prioritized my mom, especially towards the end of her life. But I ended up feeling tremendous guilt over not prioritizing my husband and sons. I also experienced stress and angst over not having enough "me time," all of which likely caused me to be short with Mom from time to time. Many of the caregivers I interviewed commented that they were short with their loved ones when they were feeling stressed. Perhaps one reason for their short fuse was this lack of self-care.

So, what's the right advice? Prioritize self-care or not? While I think everyone needs to decide the importance of self-care for themselves, I have done a lot of research on this topic and on the effects of ongoing stress. I believe it is 100 percent certain that if you don't practice self-care, you will suffer. The degree of that effect is hard to predict, but chronic stress can include negative effects to both your physical and mental health. It can result in chronic disease… and we know that caregivers experience problems with depression and anxiety.

So, make sure to take care of yourself. This may sound simple or incredibly impossible depending on your situation. Some of you work and must juggle your caregiving duties. Some of you have small children who need your focus. Some of you may not have a spouse to lean on and share duties with. There are likely dozens of personal reasons why caregiving may be negatively influencing your life, your goals, your relationships, and your plans.

And please know that self-care is personal, too. People may advise you to take a spa day, but if you aren't a spa person, don't get a massage or a facial. Maybe, for you, going horseback riding or watching a movie would be the best way to combat caregiver burnout. What's your favorite "me time" thing to do? For me, it was gardening or connecting with a friend on the phone. Do what feels best for you. *And do it early on in your caregiving journey,* maybe when you don't even feel like you need it yet.

There are also a few straightforward things you should try to fit into your caregiving day, and they are all about self-care. Keep them in mind and prioritize them.

• **Connect with one person each day (beyond your loved one and their army of doctors).** Today's technology makes this simple. Text chat with a friend or set up a weekly call (via Zoom, Skype or Facetime). Go onto a support site and chat with other caregivers who may be experiencing similar blessings or stressings. Pets are also great to cuddle with and can be a good stand-in for an actual human interaction, especially on difficult days.

• **Check in with immediate family members.** You have other "non-caregiver" roles that are important, including parent, spouse, partner, sibling, etc. Nurture these connections as part of your own self-care. You are more than a caregiver. This is something that I did not do well, and it resulted in additional stress and guilt.

• **Maintain your favorite hobby or passion.** Along with my garden retreat, I always prioritized my journal writing. Everyone needs a place to go that truly recharges them. Get your sibling to stay with mom/dad while you go play a game of tennis, if that is your passion.

• **Keep your whole family informed and provide ideas for them to help**. Some people don't realize what a caregiver spends their time doing all day, every day. They may need to be told specifically what could help (taking mom's elderly pup to the vet, dropping off some prepared meals, etc.). There are also many helpful online tools available. The *CaringBridge* (https://www.caringbridge.org/resources) is one. Tools like this can help you provide updates and caregiving needs to both local and out-of-town family members.

• **Eat healthy and resist numbing yourself with alcohol or drugs.** I can't say I always managed to resist my temptation for that glass of wine—or two—with dinner on particularly stressful days. But if you are relying on alcohol or drugs to self-medicate, know that you are risking your own health as well as the safety of your loved one.

Again, having a few lifelines can help ensure your self-care. There are adult day care services where you drop off a loved one who is elderly or suffering from dementia, so you can take a break. Often, churches have respite-focused programs and support services. Most communities have services to help with caregiving; some come to the home, and many offer sliding-scale fees.

There is a wealth of caregiving information and resources online. Check out the *Family Caregiver Alliance* (https://www.caregiver.org/caregiver-resources/health-conditions) and *American Association of Retired Persons* (https://www.aarp.org/caregiving) caregiving resources. These are two helpful websites, and there are many others associated with various medical conditions, including Alzheimer's and cancer.

Don't be a martyr and make unnecessary sacrifices. Self-care is essential to fill your cup and help manage your stress. I've heard many caregivers express regret over not asking for help earlier on.

As I mentioned, part of the self-care that I did manage to practice was keeping my journal. I've always found it helpful to write down my thoughts. Sure, some of my notes were negative and told of frustrations, stress, and sadness. But my journal writing also enabled me to capture the positives so as not to get hyper-focused on the day's challenges or future unknowns. I recommend that caregivers do this. Call it a "gratitude journal" or "positivity journal" of sorts. *What went well today? What am I thankful for?* There is usually something you can grasp onto that wasn't negative or exhausting, even on the most difficult of days.

One of the caregivers I interviewed shared a wonderful recommendation he felt was "self-care" for him: Drew took photos of his wife throughout their caregiving journey. When she was still in the early stages of her dementia, he took her to parks and gardens, and photographed her with the flowers. He took her to the zoo. He invited friends over for tea. He was sure to take at least one photo every day, which was his way of relishing the time he spent with his wife. Drew now has a wonderful memory album and beautiful photos he can admire to this day.

Truth #12: Time is often not on your side

When I was a caregiver, time was not my friend. I never had enough of it, especially during any kind of health issue with

Mom. Then, when she went into hospice, the clock to her demise started ticking. Then the coma countdown. No, time was never my friend.

Most caregivers say the same thing, that time often works against them. Running late, missing appointments, balancing caregiving time requirements with work and family, not enough "me time"—there is simply never enough time. And, unfortunately, that can make caregivers impatient and add to their stress. In my interviews, a lack of time was often cited as the major reason a caregiver began to feel overwhelmed.

Occasionally, on the way home from a doctor's appointment, we'd stop at the store, and I'd ask Mom to stay in the car while I ran in to get a prescription or other quick purchase. It was simply easier than hauling her walker out (then a ten-minute trip became closer to an hour). Later, when she was "stuck" back at the house, I'd feel bad that she wasn't able to enjoy a chance to get out and do something different. But I had saved an hour, and that seemed more important at that moment.

Katie recounted a number of times where she was abrupt with her mom and felt considerably guilty afterward. In at least one instance, her mom had ended up in tears. In hearing her stories, though, her moments of abruptness were never mean-spirited; they were simply a matter of time management in cases where her mom was dawdling when they were out and about. But as Katie remembered the scenarios, all she focused on was her own impatience and guilt.

I am an ultra-organized person, yet most weeks did not go to plan. Life was so hectic. I sometimes wonder if I could even be a caregiver today, at my older age, like many of my peers are currently doing. True, they don't have their own little ones anymore (although several now have grandkids), but in hearing them talk about their weekly caregiving schedule and routine, it now sounds a lot more daunting. However, many of them have told me that today's technology is a huge help with their time management. Alexa and Google can be helpful with any number of scheduling and task-related reminders, and I don't recall having any similar type of assistance available when I was caregiving.

Back then, my challenges with time, however, went well beyond time management. The most overwhelming concern was always the "remaining time" I had with Mom.

And finally, because I never felt like I had enough time, I felt that I had lost out on having more *quality* time with her. I wish I had done more *with* my mom instead of *for* my mom in the final year of her life. Even though I was with her most of the time in the house or yard, having meals and chats, I wish I had taken her out more often to enjoy a change in venue and each other's (non-caregiving-focused) company. She greatly enjoyed the times I managed to take her to musical events and outings. But I didn't do much of that towards the end. I never felt like I had time. We went to the doctor and to run necessary errands, and then spent most of each day at the house. After she passed away, I felt a lot of regret over not having done more of these simple things together.

Truth #13: Caregivers are not superheroes

Raise your hands if you think caregivers are only human.

Well, they are. They are not superheroes. Well, maybe to their loved ones they may seem to be. But they can't work miracles. While caregivers can do most anything to make a loved one feel they are loved and cared for, caregivers need to remember that they can't control the disease. While they might be able to control symptoms—for a while—the disease will eventually win. Remember, time is not a friend.

Caregivers can *be* there. They can *love* and show their loved one *hope*. But they can't control a loved one's deterioration over the long haul. As much as I wanted my dad to get better, he wasn't going to. As much as I wanted my mom to come out of her coma, she didn't. No matter what superpowers you may think you have, no matter how you strive to do everything with excellence and measure up to an unrealistic standard, no matter what "cures" you find online, or how much you research and plan, caregivers can't do everything.

It's important to accept there will likely be days when you don't sing, and you'll fall down the mountain, regardless of whether you're tethered to support. You may be faced with parts of the journey you simply can't traverse, either physically or mentally. You need to prepare yourself for that and be kind to yourself when it happens.

Physical strength is measured by what we can carry;
spiritual by what we can bear.
Unknown

Are you feeling guilty about thoughts of sending mom to a care home because you can no longer do it all?

Again, remember: as a primary caregiver, there is a difference between *caring* and *doing*. You may love. You may care. But at some point, sooner or later, you won't be able to do.

Those "unable to do" moments may come in increments. Today, you may need a respite day and decide to send your loved one to adult day care for the day. A month from now, you may need to incorporate day care twice a week in your caregiving calendar. At some point, you may need to find in-home care or a nursing home solution. A care receiver or family member may be unhappy—perhaps even livid—with any one of these decisions. However, a caregiver needs to know when they can no longer *do*.

One of my mom's most crushing "unable to do" moments regarding my dad was when there seemed to be no remaining viable solution that could keep him at home; thus, her decision to have him go to a nursing home. She could no longer safely care for him in their home. There was no Plan B that would work. He wasn't happy about the decision, but she could no longer *do*—only *care*.

My own "unable to do" moments with Mom? While there were many, there are three that stand out. One was when I temporarily placed her in a nursing home. One was the day she lost her mobility. And one was the challenge of moving forward after her death.

At some point, Mom developed a problem with her gastrointestinal tract. Her intestines became blocked, and it quickly became a serious health problem that needed surgery. I spent a lot of time praying to God to help her. The southern relative prayer network was up and running as well.

She always came through her various health crises with flying colors, surprising given her age and health issues. She was so petite and ate like a bird. You wouldn't think she could survive aggressive surgery like having a piece of her intestines removed, but the surgery went well. I don't think she was able to eat or drink for over a week. She was on an IV for fluids (and perhaps nutrients), and sucking on chips of ice. I was amazed at the durability of such a tiny human body, and I was shocked she survived the surgery so well. Finding out she needed postoperative medical care (including said IV) for another week after her discharge, though, was a little overwhelming. Once again, I heard a hospital administrator issue those foreboding words, "Mrs. Blum, what are you going to do?"

At the time, I was exhausted from driving back and forth, some forty miles each way, to the hospital. I was beyond worried and losing sleep. So, I am honestly not sure if I was thinking rationally at the time. I don't remember anyone suggesting I could bring her home with an in-home care nurse (needed for the IV and medication administration). All I remember is the form being waved at me and needing to know where they should discharge my mom the next day. When her doctor suggested a short-term stay at a nearby nursing home, where he was on call, as the best solution, I jumped on the idea.

Bringing her home given her medical situation was an "unable to do" moment for me. But as she was taken to the nursing home, I felt guilty. Couldn't I set-up 24-hour care in our home? Was she really going to need a nurse and IV around the clock? Had I made the right decision?

Well, Mom experienced a very difficult time in postoperative care and ended up needing much more medical care than was originally thought, so the nursing home turned out to be the best choice. She did okay for the first day or two, but then started to suffer from mental delusions. She talked gibberish non-stop, moaned and groaned, and generally appeared to be in mental and physical pain. It was upsetting to see. She was in distress, so they gave her pain meds, and her doctor visited her daily. I don't know what we'd have done had she been at home. She had to stay for a few weeks. Eventually, she got better and came home.

A friend of hers (thanks for all you meant to my mom, Jane) visited Mom in the nursing home. Thank God, I thought, someone who could see how ill she was. *Someone who could tell me I shouldn't feel guilty* about not having Mom at home.

When I communicated to my brother, Mom's friends, and our relatives that she needed to recuperate at the nursing home, they questioned me in a fairly negative, accusatory way. They only heard me say, "nursing home." The words "temporary," "recuperate," and "IV medical support" were seemingly lost. I was made to feel like the world's worst daughter.

Or was I? Did anyone really think that? Did anyone actually say that I was being selfish or uncaring? Looking back, I don't think so. Caregivers often feel conflicted emotions about not meeting everyone's expectations—including their own— when making an unpopular "unable to do" moment decision. I felt like I had let Mom down, even though I hadn't. It resulted in a self-imposed feeling of guilt and me second-guessing myself.

The second "unable to do" moment was when Mom lost her mobility. She couldn't get around well in her final years. She sometimes used a walker, but she still made it out to the dinner table. That was my benchmark for her being "okay" at the time. Her philosophy was "use it or lose it"—so she was determined to keep moving even though she had lost some of her leg strength. She even faithfully performed leg exercises.

One day, I found her in her room in front of the recliner where she watched TV. She was on the floor on her bottom. She didn't seem distressed, only embarrassed and maybe slightly surprised. She told me she simply slid off of the chair onto the ground. She might have laughed when she told me the story. I tried to help her get back up to the chair, but her legs kept buckling. We tried and tried, but to no avail. I finally lifted her back up onto the chair, and even though she was tiny, 80 pounds of dead weight was heavier than I should have lifted.

Once back on her chair, she needed to go to the bathroom, so I grabbed her portable toilet and brought it up next to her. Gathering up all of my strength, I lifted her from her chair, slid her pants down, and moved her to the toilet. When she was ready, I could barely get her back to the chair. We weren't sure at the time if this was a temporary issue or the new normal. It took another full day of needing to help her move from place to place to see that her legs were now too weak to use. Her doctor confirmed that the exercises would probably no longer help. Mom could no longer support herself or walk.

I had always thought that if Mom lost her mobility, that would be an "unable to do" moment for me. We had even talked about it a number of times. But oddly, even though I sat down with Mom a few days later to tell her so, somehow the conversation changed to, "We'll make it work." I meant to tell her, "This changes everything," but I couldn't say the words. So, we did make it work, even though it was likely a risky decision on our part.

Prior to finding her on the floor that day, it was completely clear in my mind that a lack of mobility would signal the need to move her to a nursing home. We were lucky that not adhering to that particular "unable to do" moment benchmark didn't come back to bite us. My mother could have been seriously hurt had one of us dropped her, or we might have suffered a back injury ourselves.

I think about this now when my husband or I have a bad health day—a strained back, a painful hip, or some other ailment. I think about what "unable to do" moments lie ahead for us, or those who care for us in the future. It is a great motivator to keep active and healthy.

I encourage family members to talk about what their "unable to do" moments might be, and then plan for them. Have this discussion with your loved one, and then try to adhere to what you've planned. I know it's often difficult.

Mandy said her "unable to do" moment would be when her husband, who had Alzheimer's, might endanger himself or others. Before that occurred, she'd planned to move him from their home to a specialized Alzheimer's care facility. She had earlier promised him, when he was in the initial stages of the disease, that he'd be able to remain at home, so there was a huge amount of guilt tied up in this particular decision. He was completely dependent on her for everything, including toileting. He could no longer communicate. He was waking up in the middle of the night and not going back to sleep. He eventually became belligerent, and she was concerned he might hurt himself or her, or simply walk out the door.

This plainly met her definition of her most critical "unable to do" moment, but she didn't talk to anyone about finding him a spot in an Alzheimer's facility. He continued to live at home, even though she felt it was a potentially dangerous situation for both of them.

If you know someone who is a caregiver, recognize that they may be sorting through their own set of "unable to do" moments. I'm guessing I'm not the only one who kept resetting my definition of when I needed to take action, even when friends kept telling me I needed a new plan involving more help, given my mom's lack of mobility. I didn't listen to them. They may have been right, but I couldn't accept their suggestions as options at the time. I couldn't relinquish my caregiver role and bring in 24-hour care. I couldn't accept the idea of her living alone in a nursing home.

I've heard this from other caregivers as well; an inability to even consider acting on a decision that may not be well-received by their loved one or others. Or a decision that makes a caregiver feel too great of sadness or guilt. This is yet another reason you shouldn't be climbing the mountain alone. You need others who can help you make the difficult calls. Yes, I know I didn't walk the talk on moving forward after my mom's loss of mobility. That could have ended in disaster had we dropped her. I should have listened to my friends and at least looked into additional in-home care. I don't know why I didn't.

If you see a caregiver struggling, or a care receiver at risk, it is still better to intervene with some subtle (or perhaps not-so-subtle) prodding. It could help prevent a negative or even dangerous situation from occurring. Know that they may not listen (like I didn't), but at least you will have tried.

Chapter 9

My favorite caregiving philosophies

When my mom moved in with us, and even years later, if someone had asked me how to make the caregiving journey run smoothly and be the best experience for all parties involved, I'm pretty sure the first two words out of my mouth would have been, "Have faith."

The power of faith

When I embarked on caregiving, I felt it was the right thing to do, and I was happy my life situation made it possible for me to help. I also had a lot of faith that it would work out for Mom and my family. Perhaps this is the faith that gets the climber up the mountain.

While there were many unknowns to figure out that initial year she lived with us, I never once lost the feeling that having her with us was right for my family. This belief gave me a sense of purpose, confidence, and optimism. While I didn't foresee any particular problems, I trusted that if things got difficult for whatever reason, everyone would do whatever was necessary to take corrective action. When we decided to have Mom move in with us it was truly a leap of faith—a leap that led to a beautiful nine-year journey.

Faith, of course, is also important from a religious standpoint, and was important to Mom in particular. She was a devout Catholic all of her life, so I was raised in a Catholic home, routinely went to Mass, and was even confirmed. But I "strayed" (as my mom used to put it) from attending church in my college years.

I'm fairly certain my issues with church were partially grounded in a particular priest at my parents' parish. He seemed to have a very condescending attitude about people—including his congregation. It alienated me. I thought it was odd and "un-Christian."

Or, I suppose that it could have simply been the times. It was the late '70s and there were many cultural shifts happening around me. As a very young adult, I was forming my views on a wide variety of societal concerns, and I certainly didn't agree with the Catholic Church's stance on a number of social issues that were—and still are—important to me.

While I believe in God, pray, and have held onto many religious principles throughout my life, I just wasn't a church person back then, or even now. Even so, I understood the benefit of being part of a church community. My parents' entire social support system originated from their participation in their church. I know my parents gained a lot from their religious beliefs and convictions; it guided them in their lives.

When my mother moved in with us, I wanted her to continue going to church. I wanted her to be able to practice her faith and maybe meet some members of the nearby church community. I initially told Mom I'd take her to church each week. I knew this meant going with her. It wasn't just something I said off the top of my head. I had promised that because I knew that practicing her faith was important to her.

So, the first Sunday she lived with us, we went to the local Catholic church. I hadn't been in a church for a long time—and then probably only for funerals and weddings. There was a slight smell of burning candles or incense. I remember this quite clearly because the smell of incense had always bothered me. I felt out of place, yes, but no lightning struck. I used to tell my friends lightning might strike if I went to church since I stopped attending Mass so many years prior.

The church was quite large; there were hundreds of people already sitting in the rows of pews. My mom couldn't see well, so we walked up and sat near the front. The priest began to talk during the homily. He was quite animated so I was engaged and listening. Walking around as he spoke, the priest asked a question and solicited the congregation to get some responses. His question was about a line of scripture.

I had no clue as to what the particular line was about. Others were holding up their hands, eager to respond. The priest was only about 10 feet away from me, and I felt exposed. I whispered to Mom, "If he comes over here and asks me, I'm out of here." She giggled, and had there been time for her to think about it, she might have raised my arm. But luckily, the priest went the other way, and I did not have to engage with him in front of the entire congregation. Still, I felt ill at ease.

After that initial Mass, I took Mom to church each week for several months. But sitting in that crowded church, I actually felt *less* connected to my faith. I can't explain why, but in thinking about it, I was more comfortable talking to God in the privacy and solitude of my garden. So, one day, I asked her if she'd mind if I dropped her off and picked her up instead of attending with her. She said she didn't, so that is what we did. Sometimes I'd sit with her and attend Mass, but most of the time I would walk her in, and later walk her out.

I actually don't believe my not wanting to go to church was an issue for Mom. She knew I believed in God. She knew I was a good person with a "heaven-worthy soul," as she would sometimes say. I used to laugh at that expression, but now it makes me smile.

Mom was glad to get back and forth to church until her mobility got difficult. We then asked a "mobile" priest to come by the house and give her communion. We did that for a number of years. She didn't always want me to schedule this. I assumed she was too tired on those days.

Later on, when she was in hospice in our home, I told her I'd get her the last rites. She said I didn't have to, that it wasn't something she needed; that God and she had an ongoing dialogue and He knew exactly what was on her mind and in her soul. I thought it odd how she seemed to have become disengaged from religion. It was always so important to her. I even asked her about it a few times.

I wondered if she had lost some of her beliefs or her faith. It seemed like she thought God had let her down in some way, or had let the people she loved down. One by one, her family members and friends passed away, and some experienced awful illnesses or other struggles. She sometimes commented that she didn't understand why God let bad people get a pass when so many good people did not. My dad's terrible end of life never seemed fair to Mom.

Even so, I did call in the parish priest to give her the last rites. I've always felt she was glad I did.

As a caregiver, try to "keep the faith" in your journey. Doing so will give you confidence, hope, and purpose. It can guide you through those difficult "unable to do" moments.

And don't forget that religious and spiritual care can help your loved one better accept their circumstances, as well as achieve peace and inner calm. Find a way to keep your loved one connected to their faith—even if you don't personally participate in its practices. For someone in their final weeks of life it may be the most important lifeline *they* have.

I resorted to prayer many times as Mom's caregiver. I don't know if I ever told her that, but if she is sitting on a cloud somewhere and reading this, I'm sure she is smiling and nodding her head with satisfaction. She may even be chuckling at the notion of the many "deals" I made with God at the time.

And that leads me to another caregiving jewel—you gotta have a sense of humor!

Humor is no laughing matter

You've undoubtedly heard the expression, "Laughter is the best medicine." Well, it's true. There are scientific studies supporting the idea that humor and laughter have positive benefits for both physiological and mental health. Laughter has been found to reduce systolic blood pressure as well as have beneficial effects on dementia, anxiety, and stress. It has been shown to alleviate depression and insomnia, as well as improve the sociability of older people. It may even influence the immune system by inducing natural killer cell activity.[22,23]

So, humor and laughter are good for you as a caregiver. They can help reduce caregiver stress and can strengthen your resilience and immune system—all so important given your vital role in caring for your loved one. Humor and laughter can also help you survive the worst, as well as the most embarrassing, moments of caregiving.

One day, Sarah needed to clean up after her dad, as the in-home caregiver had already left, and her dad had to go to the bathroom. The next shift's care-provider was late, leaving Sarah with no choice but to attend to her dad. It was unfortunately a number two, and he was unable to have a bowel movement (or clean up from one) without significant assistance. She initially thought this was one of her "unable to do" moments, but nothing was going to stop it from happening, so she put on some gloves and told her dad they both needed to deal with it. To distract them from the difficult and embarrassing task, she retold some of *his* worst jokes.

By the end of her story, I found myself laughing so hard that I cried. Cringing at her ordeal, but laughing at the same time. She said she and her dad also ended in laughter. She used laughter to circumvent what could have been an extremely awkward and embarrassing event.

While taking care of Mom, I helped her with a lot of things I didn't have any expertise in. Some of these turned out to be our more humorous interactions, and we often brought these memories up years later. One such incident was giving her a haircut.

I was nervous about cutting her hair, but it was getting more and more challenging to take her out for non-medical appointments. We needed to bring a walker, a wheelchair, and, later on, portable oxygen. It was cumbersome and difficult sometimes. So, I agreed to cut her hair, even though I didn't know what I was doing.

I carefully cut along the bangs and back. When I stepped back and looked, they weren't anywhere near straight. It was more like a 40-degree angle across her neck and bangs. Oh my God, I thought. I tried to even them out, which made her bangs way too short. I panicked as it got worse with each cut. I told her I needed to stop. I gave her a mirror, and she sat there moving the mirror from side to side without making a comment. Finally, I asked her what she thought. She said in her most quiet southern drawl, "I'm glad I usually wear a wig, darling!" We both buckled over laughing. She often wore a wig, but now she really, really needed to for several weeks. After that, I took her to the hair-dresser, oxygen tank and all.

Another "funny" story had to do with her toenails. One day, she told me her shoes were hurting her feet. She wore expensive orthotic shoes and didn't really walk much, so it was perplexing why her feet would suddenly be bothering her. She hadn't been to the podiatrist in a while, so I told her we'd make an appointment, as perhaps she needed her orthotics adjusted. Imagine my shock when he took off her shoes and socks, revealing these freakishly long toenails on my mom's feet. She never told me her toenails needed trimming. I'd have gladly done that. So here we were seeing a specialist, and all he did was trim her toenails. Problem solved. We laughed about this for years, especially when I trimmed her nails.

If you don't laugh, you might be horrified, or feel even guiltier. So, learn to laugh.

Expect the unexpected

A caregiver can't be prepared for every possible way the day can go wrong. When it does, however, remember how important laughter is (and don't forget to sing).

Have Plan Bs, and maybe even a few Plan Cs. Bribe your neighbors. You need a tribe looking out for you, your loved one, and your entire family. And speaking of family, *make sure you communicate* what's going on, and what has changed, to the extended family as well. Nothing disrupts family relationships more than a lack of communication, especially when followed by unexpected news about a loved one's deteriorated health status.

To keep surprises at a minimum, it is also important to know where the care receiver's journey is headed. Educate yourself if there is a particular disease (Parkinson's, cancer, Alzheimer's, etc.) or condition (dementia, incontinence, mobility challenges, etc.) involved. Know the physical changes that occur at advanced stages, and know the mental and behavioral changes to expect in the next stage as well.

Frank was caught off-guard a few times when he momentarily left a room. His wife, who had Alzheimer's and barely walked around most of the time, would suddenly get up and do something unexpected. Once, she opened up the patio door sliding window, letting an indoor-only cat out. Another time, she turned on the garbage disposal and tried to push a fork down the drain; and yet another time, she managed to lock herself in the bathroom. Although she was fine, any of these incidents could have ended with her (or the cat) getting hurt. Frank also started worrying about her turning on dangerous things like the stove.

Frank did research on the Alzheimer's support site and found solutions to ensure his wife couldn't turn on appliances; he also disconnected the garbage disposal. He removed the locks from all of the interior doors and installed floor locks on all of the sliding windows. From other caregivers on the support site, he learned there were safety latches for many items around the house that could be dangerous, including things like cabinets containing knives or glassware.

One thing that Frank wasn't aware of was "sundowning," a phenomenon that often occurs in Alzheimer's. He was left blindsided by the new and stressful nighttime behavior. He once again turned to the Alzheimer's caregiver forum for advice, only to find it is a prevalent behavior that occurs at a relatively common time in the progression of Alzheimer's. The forum had a lot of information available that was "stage" specific and helpful to know about. Frank said, "I didn't even know what to be on the lookout for until I started reading what other caregivers were dealing with. It was very helpful."

Support groups, including online forums for Alzheimer's, cancer and the like, are wonderful resources. You can learn a lot that may help you move less painfully to your loved one's next stage. Talk to their doctor. Ask questions. Be empowered. You are your loved one's best advocate.

One of the most troubling, unexpected moments in caregiving can be when a caregiver becomes incapacitated for some reason. It's important to have a backup plan for *yourself*. Do you have one? I did not.

I guess my husband and sons could have managed the day-to-day care for a few days, with my guidance, if I had been ill or something, as long as I was available at home. But if I had been gone, in the hospital or worse, there would not have been a ready alternative. I did not have a backup plan. Luckily, I never needed one, but I shudder to think what might have happened if I had been in a car accident or if something had kept me away from home for days. I never wrote out a daily plan to provide instructions for my mom's ongoing care. It had simply never crossed my mind.

There is a lot of information online that can help you create such a plan. Ideally, you should identify a backup caregiver (a family member or professional), as well as document the care receiver's health status, prescription management, medical community (doctors, labs, etc.), legal information, and the like.

A few resources you can get started with are the *American Association of Retired Persons' Family Caregiving Guide* (https://www.aarp.org/caregiving/prepare-to-care-planning-guide) and the *Family Caregiver Alliance* website (https://www.caregiver.org/resource/what-if-something-happens-to-me/).

Truth #15: Keep your friends close, but your loved one's doctor closer

I talked about the need for lifelines. Your closest friends will be your confidants, your supporters, your devil's advocates, your stress-reducers, and everything in between. Keep in contact and rely on them to help keep you at the surface so that you don't drown.

Having said that, your best friend during your caregiving journey will likely initially be an unfamiliar face—the face you see when you take your loved one to a doctor's appointment for the first time.

My parents went to the same primary care doctor for decades. That didn't change when Dad passed; Mom continued seeing their doctor, even though I felt he didn't give my dad the best care.

Dad had a skin condition throughout his adult life. His doctor prescribed a strong antibiotic (tetracycline), which my father took daily, *for years*. He got this enormous bottle of prescription antibiotics. The whole family took them when we needed to. For example, I would get recurring ear infections so out came Dad's huge bottle of pills, and I'd take them for a week. My dad's intake of all those pills, along with the toxins he was exposed to as a jet mechanic, must have had an effect on his liver and gut. They likely contributed to Dad's unexpected health decline—at least, that's always been my view.

Mom continued at the same medical practice for years. Around the time she moved from the family home, she started to have a few health issues, including her first heart attack. Her doctor kept prescribing new meds. Over time, she was on about fourteen medications, prescribed by the same doctor initially, and then prescribed by his replacement once her original doctor retired. About half she took daily; others were taken as needed. Her taking so many pills bothered me. She didn't even know why she took many of them, so I did some research. I firmly believed she was overmedicated, but her doctor didn't agree. She was so tiny and took all of those pills. I figured her system was likely overloaded, and wondered if some of the meds might have negative interactions with the others. One of my first goals as her caregiver was to get her off some of those medications.

To do that, I needed to convince her to change doctors. It took a while, but I found a geriatrics doctor—and boy, what a difference that made. The geriatrician was totally on board with decreasing her prescriptions.

I learned that about a third of adults in their sixties and seventies are prescribed five or more drugs, and there is a name for this overmedication trend: inappropriate polypharmacy. It has been well researched, with overmedication found to potentially worsen other conditions, cause cognitive impairment, or result in other adverse drug effects. It's also well known that many medications prescribed to elderly people are unnecessary.[24,25]

Mom's geriatrician believed in *deprescribing* to reduce the risks associated with too many medications. One by one, he removed medications that weren't critical. For example, Mom used a daily antibiotic for over a decade to prevent urinary tract infections. After its removal, though, she never experienced another problem. Two prescriptions were to help her sleep, but her doctor felt their potential side effects were more concerning. She was involved in the decision-making to remove a number of her medications, and she later said that she believed reducing that daily load of drugs made her feel better.

Everyone will be different of course, and please never stop providing your loved one their prescriptions without first consulting their doctor. My mom's age was definitely a factor in our decision to deprescribe some of her non-critical meds. But even if she had been younger, there are medications that can cause problems in people over sixty-five and in people taking other typical "older age" medications (related to blood pressure, heart health, diabetes, etc.). There are a number of resources available to learn more about polypharmacy, including the *American Geriatrics Society Beers Criteria® for Potentially Inappropriate Medication Use in Older Adults*. Here is an overview by the *Cleveland Clinic* (medically reviewed by the site as of 2023) of how the Beers Criteria can help your loved one's doctor evaluate the deprescribing of some of their medications. (https://my.clevelandclinic.org/health/articles/24946-beers-criteria).

Mom's "inappropriate polypharmacy" was over a decade ago. With today's technology, pharmacies may have taken a more active role in flagging drug interactions and over-medication that can be hazardous to the elderly or chronically ill. Having said that, I've heard from other caregivers that their loved ones were typically on over a dozen drugs, so I wonder if much has changed.

My mom's geriatrician (thank you Dr. L) became my lifeline, and years later, he helped me transition her to hospice. I truly believe that finding him was a major positive for Mom's quality of life. I hope he realizes how helpful he was, making her later years good ones, and mine as well.

Truth #16: You won't know everything

I did a lot of things right in caring for my mom, but I made many mistakes as well, and I'm not simply talking about toenails and haircuts.

One particular mistake that stands out is related to apple juice and applesauce. You wouldn't think either of these could cause someone so much discomfort—even pain—but it did. I erroneously thought a good way to deal with Mom's constipation was to give her apple juice and applesauce (lots of it). Prior to reducing her prescription load, she would get stopped up as a side effect of so many medications. Who knew all that apple juice could actually cause other digestive issues and discomfort? I surely didn't.

After weeks of trying to "help" her, and her experiencing incredibly painful bloating, I finally reached out to her doctor and learned that too much apple juice and applesauce was the culprit. Good job, Dr. Blum.

Caregivers often research a given disease hoping to find a supplement or vitamin that will help, but most of the time, these "miracle cures" have little or no evidence supporting their claimed benefits, and can sometimes cause problems.[26]

Suzanne read an article about how vitamins could help improve Parkinson's, so she loaded up her husband with vitamin-enriched supplements. His doctor later vetoed them. Mandy gave her husband a holistic potion for dementia that she found on the internet. It turned out to contain ingredients that were not compatible with his medications. Several of the caregivers I interviewed changed their loved one's diet after reading an article on how a given diet could prevent or cure dementia or the particular disease of the care receiver. The diets often restricted one thing or the other, including protein, carbs, fats, etc. In some instances, the restricted diets aggravated a care receiver's existing symptoms.

I'm not saying not to trust your gut and make calls, and I do know there is research showing that specific diets and nutrients can be helpful for certain diseases and conditions. But realize that taking care of someone doesn't make you a medical authority, and doesn't mean you shouldn't ask questions.

Make sure you are evaluating things on reputable sites (like the national Alzheimer's site, American Cancer Society, etc.) or using reputable research sites (PubMed is one I use), then discuss your findings with your loved one's doctor *prior* to implementing any health-related changes.

You will make mistakes. All caregivers do.

Join their journey

Back to other caregiving jewels. One I really love is: "You need to join your loved one's journey." It's especially true in situations involving dementia or Alzheimer's, but it is a good philosophy for any caregiving situation. It means that you need to change your perspective to match that of the person you are caring for.

When my mom was accepted into "hospice" and became eligible for outside services, I thought, "How great, she can have all of these different resources that will come to our home and interact with her." First, a woman with a guitar came out. My mother loved music. Then we scheduled a massage therapist, but having a massage hurt Mom. She didn't like it at all. Next, a volunteer came and read poetry to her. There was even a guy with a bongo drum. There were several weeks of visitors.

One day, Mom said, "I really don't want these people coming to see me anymore; some of them are really strange." I realized then that I needed to get a clearer perspective of what she wanted to do in her final days. As it turned out, it wasn't to be "entertained" by a series of random people. After that, I always asked her what she wanted to do, and didn't simply schedule things to fill her days. More often than not, she wanted to hang out at home and listen to music, watch TV, be with our family, or talk to relatives and friends on the phone. That was what made her happy.

Drew said his wife started hoarding as her Alzheimer's progressed. It initially confused him, and then annoyed him. He'd find all kinds of garbage tucked away in closets—at one point, he even found discarded food items covered in ants. He wasn't aware that hoarding is a very typical behavior of the condition. Once he joined his wife on her journey and understood that she couldn't control the urge and that it was a normal progression of the disease, he simply learned to remove the garbage more often and keep it out of her reach. He was no longer irritated by the behavior. Problem solved.

Katie wanted to send her mom to adult day care. Not so much for her own respite, but she thought her mom was too socially isolated. However, the reality was that her mom loved being at home in a familiar, comfortable, and safe setting. She liked being around the family pets, the garden, and her daughter. Katie said, "I was initially trying to figure out a plan for her that I would have liked for myself. I wouldn't want to be stuck at our house, for example. The painting class at the adult day care seemed like a great idea until I stopped and thought about it from my mom's perspective. For her, it was taking her out of her favorite place, making her interact with strangers, and do things she wasn't interested in."

I took Mom to a number of adult day care facilities to check them out. She was very friendly and artistic, so I thought she'd like to meet people and do crafts, etc. But after we toured a few, she was uncharacteristically negative about them. I couldn't understand why. But slowly, I realized she viewed these as more work for me (getting her there, picking her up). I also don't think she felt as isolated as I thought she was. She still enjoyed her weekly Lunch Bunch gatherings and seeing other infrequent visitors, and that was "enough" for her. I was looking at her life through my younger eyes. She was too tired to do the things I had planned for her.

A caregiver needs to stop and think about their loved one's daily journey from the care receiver's perspective. What are their fears? What makes them feel safe and comfy? What puts them in their happy place?

Live in the day

Yesterday is gone. Tomorrow has not yet come.
We have only today. Let us begin.
Mother Teresa

Similar to matching the perspective of your loved one, it is helpful not to focus on the past or future, but to be present in the day at hand. The past may be full of missteps or guilt. The future is uncertain. So, focus on the small positives of each day.

Even someone with advanced Alzheimer's may show signs of their remaining personality—perhaps a smile may appear when hearing music. *You merely have to stay present so you don't miss them.*

Years ago, I wrote caregiving-focused blogs for the Alzheimer's Association, and I was invited to one of their enrichment programs focused on artwork. It was called, *"Memories in the Making."* People with Alzheimer's created art pieces, and the event honored them and their work. It was quite impressive. The artwork was set up like an art gallery, and each piece had a brief description of what the artist had drawn. Many pieces were depictions of the artists' long-ago childhood homes, drawn in such vivid details. It was fascinating to see how people could tap into distant memories that evoked strong feelings for them.

After looking at the displays, we sat down for lunch with the artists and their families. Many were in advanced stages of Alzheimer's and couldn't communicate. Some sat and rocked quietly in their chairs. Some needed to be fed by their caregivers. I was a little uncomfortable, as I had never been around anyone at an advanced stage of the condition. I wasn't sure what to do or say.

At the end of the lunch, Big Band-type songs began to play. Imagine my surprise and delight when a woman at our table, quietly rocking—and not eating or talking the entire time— sprang up, grabbed her husband's hands, and took to the dance floor. Her previously expressionless face lit up, all smiles, all delight, truly joyous. Her husband, too, was relishing that *single moment*; one of few they could still both enjoy.

I mentioned regretting not spending more "non-caregiving" time with my mom. We went to the dentist with her portable oxygen tank in tow, so why didn't we go to lunch or a movie? Or a public garden, or any number of places available for us to enjoy together? While Mom lived a happy life, I was so focused on caregiving schedules and "to-dos" that I missed out on many opportunities to simply be present and enjoy her company.

While it can be difficult, try to create positives each day, and be present for your loved one. Don't just grieve for all the losses. Don't focus solely on the inevitable future.

Truth #17: You sometimes need to say "no"

Yes, don't dwell on the future, but definitely do things to make the future easier. Along with doing a little research on your loved one's disease—to know what's coming—one of the best words of advice I have is to learn to say "no."

During my caregiving years, I was also a mother of two young sons, a wife, a freelance writer and consultant, a volunteer at my kids' school and Scouts, a homemaker, and a friend. That's a lot, and many of you likely have several other "titles" that you hold and devote your time and energy to on top of caregiving. Caregivers are busy, and often overly so.

When asked to take on more, there is power and self-care in saying "NO!" You don't have to yell it, of course; you can say it without the caps and exclamation mark. There were many opportunities for me to say "no"—particularly regarding the volunteering I was doing at my kids' schools and in Scouts. No one would have cared. So why didn't I do it more often?

I think it's that caregiver guilt thing again, wanting to do it all. After all, caregivers have superpowers, right?

No, we really don't.

Once you've learned you have no superpowers, and that you can't possibly do it all, you may even opt to say "no" to your loved one. Not "no" to being their caregiver, perhaps, but maybe you'll define some limits of what you more realistically can do.

Libby took on the primary caregiving for her mother after her father had died. Her mother was in an early stage of Alzheimer's. Libby worked full time at a job that also involved travel, so she sat down with out-of-state family members and had a frank conversation about what she could and could not do. She worked at home, but she could not stop traveling and stay employed. There were a number of areas of responsibility where she offered a polite but firm "no." Fortunately, with this advanced family planning, they all worked out a plan that kept their mother at home with Libby. The siblings said "yes" to working out a schedule to cover their sister's travel and to help pay for some daytime caregiving assistance so that Libby could focus on her work.

I do recall getting better at saying "no" in Mom's later years. But it did take me a while to accept that caregivers oftentimes have to make hard choices to give time to one person and not the other. Remember that caregivers are not superhuman. If only we could clone ourselves!

The power to say "no" is important. Don't be a caregiver who says "I had no choice." While some may find that is true, explore your options and possibilities. Say "no" when you feel it's important, and see what is workable.

Chapter 10

What is quality of life?

For most of the time that Mom lived with us, her health was relatively stable. Sure, she had recurrent health emergencies relating mainly to her heart, but in general, she recuperated quickly from these events, experienced few adverse health symptoms or pain, and did quite well over the many years.

She was determined to stay mobile, healthy, and at home with us. One of her benchmarks for health was walking up the hill on our street. She walked almost every day, weather allowing. Our block wasn't that long, but there was a relatively steep section in the middle. Many people huffed and puffed when they hit that part of the walk. Mom slowly made her way up that hill, sometimes stopping and leaning on a fence or a tree, even sitting on a fire hydrant—but she eventually made it all the way up and then walked to the end of the street. The entire walk might have been only about 200 yards from our house, but it was her own little fitness tracker.

The neighbors often commented on this journey: a tiny woman who looked quite frail, in her late eighties and then nineties, making it up that steep section of the hill. They found it quite inspiring.

I knew that something was off with her if she did not go for that walk on a good weather day. And yes, one time she didn't walk due to those frightfully long toenails.

She also liked taking a short walk around our street, a dead-end circle, sometimes stopping to watch the kids playing. Early on, she often attended our neighborhood functions, including an annual BBQ and Christmas party. She was very vibrant—loved to sing Christmas carols and was a wonderful singer. Most of the neighbors knew her, and she knew them. That was comforting to me.

Resting in our neighborhood prior to taking her walk

It wasn't until her final year or so that she stopped those walks up the hill. She started using a walker around the house and a wheelchair when we were out and about; then she completely lost her mobility toward the end.

136

Even with reduced mobility, she still enjoyed many social interactions, both on the phone and with visitors. She talked a lot with my brother and his three kids. His two daughters came out several times from the East Coast to visit, with or without their father. Their Granny loved seeing them, and I know they enjoyed spending time with her as well. I'm quite sure her five grandkids were one of the reasons Mom was so determined to keep going.

I think she'd have said she lived a good, quality life. I believe she was happy, and I know she was thankful she didn't lose any of her mental capacities along the way. She often commented on how terrible it would be not to remember one's life and one's family. She only lost her mental sharpness in her final weeks of life, due primarily to pain medication.

People loved her, cared for her, and reached out to her, including many longtime friends, the Lunch Bunch, and extended family. When she moved in with us, I initially worried she might be socially isolated. We lived far from most of her friends and the community she was living in for some time. But it had worked out great.

Time passed, and then one day, our youngest son found his Granny on the floor of her bathroom. She had toppled over and was out of it, so we took her to the hospital. It wasn't a heart attack, but she had gotten dizzy. They released her the next day and home she came, but she never seemed as content after that.

I wondered if it was one hospital stay too many for her. I tried to rally her by having friends come by and arranging for relatives to call, but she pretty much sat and watched TV. Even her body language was off. She sat slumped on her recliner and didn't engage.

Chapter 11

Failure to thrive

Weeks went by, and Mom was not getting better. She was always so strong for such a fragile little thing and had continually possessed the attitude that she wasn't going to let her body defeat her. But this time, things were different. She was lethargic and quiet. She seemed to have lost interest in pretty much everything. I tried to talk to her about it, but she said little that pointed me toward what was going on. She also said little to others she spoke to. She started declining friends' phone calls, saying she didn't feel up to talking.

I called her doctor and said I was worried. Had she given up? He labeled it "failure to thrive" and suggested hospice in our home.

Failure to thrive. I wasn't exactly sure what that meant. And hospice was a scary word, as it meant imminent death. In talking with her doctor, it was clear he thought she was in her final few months. The truth is, I felt that she probably was. But I didn't want to accept that.

The doctor filled out the forms so she could enter this thing called hospice. A hospice administrator contacted me the next day and set up a visit. She asked a bunch of questions, including whether my mom had an advanced directive. The administrator was so abrupt. "Does your mom have a 'do not resuscitate' on the advanced directive?" Wow, nice to meet you too, and glad you care so little about my mom *living*. Well, I know she was only doing her job. Mom did indeed have the "do not resuscitate" (DNR) in her advanced directive. I wasn't sure I would find that easy to honor, but I understood it was her wish.

One comment on the advanced directive, by the way. Your care receiver should have one (you should, too), and you need to discuss it with them well in advance of needing to use it. Mom was ninety-three and ready to go. She didn't want to be in pain or in a nursing home. She'd already lost her mobility. So, her choice to not prolong her life with nourishment or medications (other than for pain) was an easy decision *for me to accept*. True, the advanced directive itself will tell the hospital and doctors what to do, but it's still important that *you* understand what's been stipulated *by your loved one*. For someone younger, or with less obvious health complications, it might be more difficult for you to accept what you or others may have to do—or *not do*. Find information on advanced directives, including a planning guide and where you may be able to find free forms, at the *National Institutes of Health (NIH), National Institute on Aging (NIA)* website. (https://www.nia.nih.gov/health/advance-care-planning/advance-care-planning-advance-directives-health-care).

So, we made the appointment, and the following day, a nurse came to meet my mom, who was suddenly in a place called hospice.

140

Chapter 12

A place called hospice

I learned that hospice wasn't necessarily an imminent end of life. Mom was in hospice for much longer than the few months they had predicted.

Hospice was a wonderful place, and I encourage others to not be afraid of it. It enabled Mom to easily get medications, have her vitals checked, and talk to a nurse, without leaving our home. It gave me a more direct route to the doctor for medical questions. It brought in a hospital bed and other equipment that helped her considerably. It made things less complicated, and made me feel safer and more supported.

True, I kind of went crazy with the other service opportunities, like the musician and poet. But once I figured all that out, I valued the medical attention my mom could so effortlessly get. The nurse came weekly but could be consulted any time. The hospital bed, while initially foreboding, was very helpful. When she needed oxygen, *poof...* an oxygen machine appeared.

Mom seemed to do better after being put on hospice. Perhaps it was wishful thinking on my part. Or it could have been due to the oxygen throughout the night. But she definitely seemed happier. I sometimes wonder if hospice, and what it signaled, brought her some peace.

She wore diapers by now. I handled any needed personal care, but the hospice in-home care provider came in the morning and helped Mom shower. Kato carried my mother to a shower chair, bathed her, and shampooed her hair. Kato was such a blessing—so strong yet so gentle. She was from the Pacific Islander community, and I learned that there were many such women in valued caregiving roles.

After a few hours, I'd stop in and Mom would be back in bed, in clean clothes and looking so sweet. She was always so pleasant and thanked Kato for everything she did. After her shower and breakfast, I'd usually get her on the phone with a friend or relative. Those were her favorite moments, as the phone took her out of her bed and into the homes of her friends and loved ones.

She would usually talk to a few people and then get very tired, often opting for a TV program, or maybe a nap. Those were the days of hospice. We didn't really go anywhere, as we didn't have medical appointments. I spent a lot of time with her. Most of it was still centered around caregiving tasks, but we often looked at photo albums and chatted about her grandkids—my two sons (Chris and Casey) and my brother's two daughters (Jenny and Melissa) and son (Eddie)—and what was going on in their lives. She was very proud of them.

During this time together, Mom wanted to plan her funeral. For years, she had kept a file folder with prayer cards, poetry verses, and songs that she liked. I finally relented, and we spent days going through her folder, picking out a few songs and some scripture. It made me sad and a little anxious, but it clearly contented her. We discussed her desire to be cremated. My dad had been cremated, and she was to be buried with him at the National Cemetery (as he was a veteran) in San Francisco. She slyly said, "Put me on top of him, he'll like that." My mom was so funny. I laughed, but that is what we eventually did. We put her urn on top of his for eternity.

After initially seeming better, she began to grow weaker. Her doctor knew this might happen, but it was stressful to see. She also started to have pain in her hip. We suspected that she might have hurt it in a fall, but her doctor didn't want to make her go for X-rays, as there wasn't anything they could do given her state of health. He recommended pain medication.

People told me that pain meds are the kiss of death for the elderly. I understood what they meant, but I didn't want her to be in pain. So, we started the medications. They helped, but yes, they made her foggy, and it became difficult for her to have a quiet night's sleep. She experienced vivid dreams and often tried to get out of bed, which could have resulted in another fall. I bought a baby monitor for her room, and every night I'd hear her trying to pull herself up out of the bed. I'd run to her room and try to get her to go back to sleep.

Then one night, she fell. I heard it on the baby monitor—an exclamation followed by a thud. I ran down and pulled her back into bed. The only injury I could see was a bump on her head. She seemed okay, but I called the doctor to be safe. The next day, the hospice nurse checked her out and said she was alright, although her bump had developed into some pretty scary bruising. I felt so bad for Mom.

After that, we put ties across her waist at night to keep her from getting up. They were loosely tied so I knew it didn't hurt her, but it was sad to see. Every night, I'd hear her attempt to get up. It sounded like scratches, but the ties appeared to work. She was safely tucked into bed every morning, although sometimes wedged in a corner.

Occasionally, while I was talking to her, she'd suddenly look to her right or left, then she'd quietly ask me if I saw the fairy go by. I hadn't, of course, but asked her if it was a friendly spirit, and she said it was. That made me smile.

Her condition worsened, although she didn't seem to be in pain. She wasn't eating much. The doctor said he didn't think she would be around much longer. I started to send updates to close family. I wasn't sure what people wanted to know, but I felt it was easier to send an email to a distribution list. I subsequently heard from several relatives that these emails, while informative, were difficult for them to receive, especially after Mom fell into a coma. Here are a few from when my mom was in the later days of hospice.

Diane's journal: Hospice and morphine

Wanted to let people know that things are not good at all with my mom. I feel she will go any day now. I am sorry to have to tell you all that. A few days ago, she could no longer support her weight at all, even with help. Now she has pretty much stopped eating. She can barely swallow but is still drinking juice. She is not in pain. She is confused a bit; I think it is due to the morphine. We have been telling old stories; she has still been managing to smile and even laugh. We have been talking about my dad. My mom still finds it so hard to believe that she outlived him by some fifteen years. Thanks to all for your support, kindness and prayers.

And then…

My mom is hanging in there but is pretty much sleeping. The morphine cuts the pain, but I think they are going to have to increase the dosage. If they do, I'm fairly certain she won't be overly "lucid" after that. She is already having hallucinations, mainly about relatives visiting. I think she blurs phone calls with reality. I wake her up to eat, although she barely eats. It is not a good existence. She is getting very confused about the time of day, etc. She has always had her mind, so that is hard for her and all of us. Thanks to everyone for being so attentive, she loves getting the phone calls, even if she misses them (I still play the machine for her).

And later…

I wanted to send an additional message; hope you enjoy gallows humor. Last night, my mom kept trying to get out of bed, three times throughout the night she tried, and three times I found her in a state of being "wedged" in some corner of the bed. I have her on a baby monitor so I hear her crying out; luckily in each instance, I heard her. This morning, I heard a rooster crow, over and over again. I woke up thinking, what the heck is that? Well, she got this thing from an organization for the blind that tells her the time when she pushes a button, and she was pushing it over and over. It says the time out loud but also has a rooster crow. I heard it over and over and over (there must have been like seven rooster crows, one after another), so went down to check on her. Clearly, she thought it was a "call nurse" type button in a hospital. When I got there and asked her what was wrong, she said (as she kept pushing the button), "Isn't there anybody on this floor to help me?"

When she had a clear day, we would continue with the funeral planning. I sent this email update after one such session.

We sat for an hour today and went through a folder containing poems/songs/scripture she liked from other people's funerals. It was hard for me, but I felt at great peace talking with her about what she wanted.

I want you all to know that she specifically commented how wonderful it made her feel that she was so cared about, and much of that was relatives... you. She said, no matter what she had in terms of money or possessions, that the most important thing was that she mattered to people, and she realized that she really did matter, and not only to her immediate family, but to so many others, and that people cared.

In particular, she commented on Cornelia, a "daughter" to her, in many regards. And Susan, "another daughter" who has been so wonderful to her and who she has so many wonderful weekly lunches with, and to Allie Boo, who (along with Claire) has made her feel so special, and Rosemary, who has gone out of her way to keep in touch, and Eddie, who has so inspired her, and his brother Joe, who has made her feel totally special given he calls her from Japan, and Sally and others. Don't feel bad if I haven't mentioned you, as I am so completely tired and am unable to remember all her thoughts and comments.

I apologize if some of this is rambling. I didn't get a lot of sleep last night and felt the need to send an email.

Thanks to you all. You have made my mom's last days quite wonderful. She told me today that she was so blessed, so many phone calls and so many people caring. Thank you and I will try and keep you posted.

Chapter 13

Last rites and angels

Late in hospice, I asked Mom if she wanted the last rites. She said no. As mentioned earlier, Mom was a very religious person her entire life, so that caught me by surprise.

But she also was very progressive for a woman in her nineties. She'd often comment on the news, especially regarding human rights and any number of social matters. She seemed to take issue with the Pope himself on many politicized topics, including the church's marginalized treatment of the gay community. She was also horrified by the molestations happening within the clergy.

While she had certainly expressed these concerns over the years, I never viewed them as an inhibitor to her faith. So, when she started canceling the priest's visits to bring her communion at the house, I didn't think too deeply about it. But for her to say she didn't want the last rites was unexpected. I thought about it for a while, and asked her again. She still said no. She said she wasn't that keen on religion given all that was going on in the world. But I felt it was something she needed. So, I went out on a limb and called the parish priest. He said he'd come Friday night. On Thursday, I told Mom he was coming the following day. She seemed very surprised, but then said in a very soft voice, "Thank you."

The next day, I was so stressed out. Mom was fading, and I wanted to make sure she was going to be conscious when the priest came. Finally, he arrived. The priest introduced himself, came in, and without much explanation or fanfare, gave my mom the last rites. It was very quick. And I kid you not, after the priest left, she asked, "Is that it?" Later that night, a neighbor—who was quite religious—came over. My mom told her she received the last rites and it was a little underwhelming. The neighbor said, "What were you expecting, the angels flying you up to heaven?" Mom responded, "That would have been nice!"

The following day, Mom thanked me again and said she was glad I had arranged for the priest to come, even though the last rites were not exactly what she had envisioned. In the end, it was important to her, a lifelong Catholic.

In her final weeks of hospice, I wrote a lot in my journal, grappling with so many emotions and deep sadness. I knew I was about to lose her, and that was an unfathomable thought. I would not only lose my mom but also this special friend with whom I had shared an intimate relationship over the past several decades. I'd have done anything for her, to make her days more special, anything to keep her with us a little longer.

And I knew she was appreciative. I knew she felt cared for and loved. Her daughter loved her. Mom used to say how surprised she was at how well everything had turned out and that she never knew how strong I was. I'd say, "It is you that is strong." It was a special mom and daughter bond on top of the caregiving bond.

At one point, while my mom was in hospice, I wrote the following in my journal. I shared it with many friends at the time, as so many of them were in caregiving roles of their own. I had been thinking about the mom-daughter caregiving relationship and the fact that I didn't have a daughter. Remember, my family script—and that of my friends—was very much that the daughter of the family eventually took on the caregiving responsibilities for her parents.

Diane's journal: I should have had at least one daughter

It was during a panic attack late last night when I realized that I should have had at least one daughter.

In that dark moment, I had been reflecting on my own life as a daughter, and on my mom, now in hospice, with only months to live.

My mom, now ninety-three, moved in with my family some nine years ago after suffering several heart attacks while living alone. I vividly remember camping out in her small apartment, on the floor in a sleeping bag, during her recovery from one of those illnesses. I remember driving back and forth, hurried hour-long trips, between my ailing mom and my then young family.

I said "goodbye" to my mom more times than I can remember
back then. A daughter, at her mom's side, in a hospital, holding
her mother's hand. This scene played out over and over again. A
kiss on the forehead, a pat on the head, and a reassuring
voice. Not ever really ready to say goodbye, but having to say it
just the same.

Later, I was a daughter taking her mom for a follow-up blood
test, walking into yet another waiting room full of other
daughter-mom duos. We would exchange knowing glances, us
daughters; a meek smile, acknowledging each other's role. I
remember thinking more than once how tired those daughters
looked. How worried. How defeated even, sometimes. I never
thought—not even for a minute—that perhaps they were
thinking the same thing about me.

I have sometimes told my sons—to explain some feat I have just
performed on their behalf— "It is a mom thing." We moms
seem all-knowing; we can be creative at the drop of a hat with
only a paper plate, a glue stick, and crayons. We can pull just
about anything that is vital at a moment in time, out of our
purses. We always have snacks. We juggle a seemingly complex
set of schedules for our active kids. We volunteer. It is in our
genes; that is the only explanation.

I think there is a similar gene in daughters. Daughters can
perform miracles for their aging moms. They can take a moment
of horror, bend it slightly, and make it a moment of either
humor or nothingness. Daughters can overlook so much; yet
they can see with great clarity. A daughter can do so many of
the most important things for an aging mom, and even more for

152

a dying mom. A daughter knows when to talk and when to stop. When to intrude on privacy and when that privacy must be honored.

Many years pass. Many 911 calls, many trips to the ER. More "goodbyes." Prayers, always followed by relief. More follow-up appointments. I never minded. I wanted to be there to help comfort and care for my mom. I love her.

Perhaps part of me was there out of a daughter's sense of duty as well. And sometimes, it was just life unfolding. No time to think, just enough time to respond. But there was great joy as well. Many, many good days. A bond was created between my mom and my sons, which will be with my two boys forever. I relish the nine years, so many wonderful memories. I relish the relationship I've had with my mom.

More recently, my mom's health has deteriorated and I suddenly am in a new place. The place is called hospice. It is all about comfort, not recuperation. Previous independence disappears one day, and I am suddenly back in that "newborn baby" caregiver mode. But the baby is ninety-three years old. Still, I love this baby dearly, and want to care for her.

But it is hard. There are other trade-offs now; my own family must fend for itself, my attention elsewhere. The family calendar is outdated; appointments get missed; schedules forgotten. We are tethered to our home, not being able to leave, at least, not all of us, together. With each passing day, a new pain, a new dependency, a new indignity arises.

New medications come along to bring comfort. The comfort comes with a price. A sharp mind is replaced with confusion. A strong wit with tears and despair. New challenges for my mom crop up in doing every day, simple things. New reasons for me, a daughter, to cry in frustration. New reasons to lash out at random things.

One day, I am trying to cash some bonds for her and the broker wants my dead father's social security number. He has been dead for fourteen plus years, so the social security number is not to be found. It is buried somewhere, in old paperwork filed away long ago. I search and search, and suddenly find myself flinging files around the room, so angry. I am crying to this stranger on the phone. Don't they understand? I am a daughter and my mother is dying.

Suddenly, you realize there isn't enough time. There isn't enough time to live your life and care for your dying mother.

Not enough time. It reminds me of how I felt with my first newborn. So exhausted, so "bound" by such a simple creature. Each day blurring into the next. No spontaneity, simply a series of caregiver tasks. Feeding, diapering, giving a bath, and then feeding again, and the process cycles on and on, and the day fades into the night. I loved my baby, but it was hard; everything revolved around that little creature's needs. It is like that now, for this daughter, with my mom. A series of caregiving tasks. Medicine, meals, replace the oxygen tubing, helping her to bed and back up again, words of comfort, and the cycle goes on.

But there came a time when that newborn took a step. For my aging mom, there are few steps left. I sometimes envision a

154

stairway for her to heaven. In her present body, she can't walk up even a couple of stairs. She can barely walk. But in her future heavenly body, I like to think she will bound up the stairs, two at a time. She will be pain-free.

I am not sure what I believe about death, but perhaps she will be reunited with my dad, her many siblings, maybe even her own mom. Somehow, that thought brings a measure of peace. Knowing she will be out of pain brings even more calm to an otherwise unthinkable thought.

It will be hard to lose her. Her room in my home for nine years will become so still and cold. She hates the cold. So, everything there now is cozy and warm. Blankets, comforters, electric heating pads. A heat massager. Fuzzy socks. Only a daughter would have bought all of those things. Only a daughter would make hot tea and a hot breakfast every single morning, even on those mornings when there really wasn't enough time.

I have two wonderful sons, teenagers. They love me and their dad, and they love my mom. They don't really believe me when I tell them she is dying. They know it, but they don't believe it. Their eyes try to avoid the inevitable signs. They will be sad. I try to talk with them about death, but they will have no part of it.

They are good sons. The younger one recently told me, if their dad wasn't still alive and around to take care of me, that I could come live with him when I am old. That makes me laugh, yet, I reflect on it. I love my son. He loves me, but he is a son. He doesn't know how to do it all. He doesn't have the gene! And when the cycle brings me to that place, where I am old and frail, I think about how much I will need a daughter. And thus, last night's panic attack. I really should have had at least one daughter.

But life, at least for now, goes on. I listen to the rhythmic pulsing of my mother's oxygen machine; it almost sounds soothing. The tubing, like an umbilical cord, bringing her the nourishment she needs to survive. The cycle continues. A kiss on the forehead, a pat on the head, and a reassuring voice. Not ever really ready to say goodbye, but having to say it just the same.

I wrote this over fifteen years ago, when my sons were teens. They are two loving, caring sons, and now that they are young adults, I have seen firsthand that they do have the "gene." I can only hope that this is partly due to the family script my husband, our family, and I passed down to them and nurtured throughout their lives. I'm so proud of the young men they have become.

Chapter 14

A good death

I have always said that my mom's death was as good as one could ask for.

First, she had her mind completely; she never experienced dementia. She only got a little foggy at the end due to pain medications. That's when she saw her fairies. But then again, perhaps they were really there, flitting around her—angels arranging for my mom's final journey to see her God.

Second, she didn't have a lot of pain toward the end, and we were liberal with pain medication when she did. She slipped into a coma one day, and a week later, peacefully passed away.

And third, she knew she was dying well before she actually did. We took that time to talk and cherish what time was left. She planned her own funeral, we looked at old photo albums, and we talked and talked. It was a very special, intimate time with her.

She got to say her goodbyes to the important people in her life. And when she went into her coma, she had flowers by her bedside, her favorite music playing on her CD player, and her favorite PJs on along with her favorite fuzzy socks. Some days, her daughter was curled up next to her, reading to her.

Yes, it was a good death. But for the living? It wasn't so good.

Chapter 15

Our medical crisis trifecta

Hospice continued for months, and with each passing day, we knew we were getting closer to the end.

Several times, Kato brought up the topic of my mom's eventual passing. She was trying to determine how much longer this job with Mom was going to last, but asking in a kind, loving manner. Kato seemed to have an uncanny sense of caregiving and end-of-life concerns. I had been so impressed with and thankful for the care and comfort she had provided to my mother.

A few weeks prior, Kato had said she didn't think my mom would be around past another week or so, which was where we were now. Then one morning, she mentioned again that she thought Mom was nearing her end. I didn't think about the specific timeframe, really. I knew my mom was dying… but later on, it occurred to me that both her doctor and Kato had the timeline pretty well figured out.

The next day, in the middle of the night, we were abruptly awakened by my husband's mom calling. Gramma was dizzy and in distress. My husband went to pick her up and bring her to our home, but ended up going to the ER. She thought she was having a heart attack. The doctors declared it vertigo. They came back to our house around 4:30 the next morning.

When my mother-in-law woke up later, she felt fine. She chatted briefly with Mom before the care provider came for her shift. Since Kato was going to be there for a few hours, I drove Gramma home. The minute I was back at our house, my husband called from work. I thought he was checking on his mom, so I launched into, "She's fine, but she needs to go back to the doctor." He cut me off and said, "My dad just died."

Later that night, I sent an email out to my family.

Diane's journal: Another death

My mom is hanging in there, but her energy is really diminishing. She is very peaceful, though.

Much less peaceful is what else is going on around here.

John's mom fell ill last night and he took her to the hospital. They came in at 4:30 in the morning (she came home with him and slept on the couch). The doctors said it was vertigo but that she should be okay. I took her home this morning. Then when I got home John called and said his dad (in Florida) had died unexpectedly.

Unbelievable. His dad's wife (John's stepmom) died very recently a few months ago, also unexpectedly. Then his dad was diagnosed a few weeks ago with terminal lung cancer, but they said it would be a slow end; gave him like a year or so. But he

160

experienced some kind of blood clot, and they called an ambulance, and he died en route. John is in complete shock; he thought there was time for us to visit his dad this summer. It is very shocking to me as well, on top of everything else. What is going on?

So, my husband needed to fly to Florida the next day.

I went into my mother's room. She was having a perky day. She was freshly showered and back in her red flannel PJs— "snug as a bug," she would say. Kato said she enjoyed an especially good morning. I told Mom about John's dad, and she was very sad for him. To cheer her up, I told her I'd call a few relatives, including one of her nieces who had called earlier. Sally and Mom spoke for a while, and my mom was very animated and energetic. She also spoke to my brother. She was unusually spunky.

After that call, I thought I'd try to reach her brother Jimmy, who had also called my mom earlier. They had something of a running gag about who would be the last sibling alive out of a very large family. They were the last two of nine. But he didn't answer his phone. I tried a few other people, but no one was available, so I told her we'd try Jimmy again later. Kato left, and my cousin Susan stopped by to visit. Mom was getting tired, so Susan tucked her in and said something about taking a nice nap and dreaming of angels. My mom replied that she'd love to see some.

Later, when I went in to wake Mom up, she didn't open her eyes. I jiggled her but got no reaction. I tried several more times, but still no reaction. She did not wake up. I called the hospice nurse who came out to check. Yes, Mom was in a coma. I told her how energetic my mother was earlier in the day; the nurse said that was very common, that people often rally right before they go into a coma or pass away.

I called Kato later that night and told her Mom was in a coma. She wasn't surprised by the news. She said she felt it was time given my mom's energy surge. She also said she didn't think it would be long before my mom passed, given her weak state.

I told Kato she didn't need to come back. Given my mom's frail condition, and Kato's prediction that Mom wouldn't last long, I guess I assumed she'd pass very quickly. But we'd soon find out that my sweet little mom wasn't quite ready to go.

Diane's journal: Mom is dying

At the end of each day, I sent an email to our relatives. I jotted down notes in my journal as well. They were all pleadings for God to take this little angel, and cries of despair over His not taking her yet.

The emails were difficult for my relatives to read. I didn't know that at the time, but given my emotional state and lack of sleep, they were often too informative, emotional, or rambling. Besides, there was nothing that any of them could really do.

They couldn't be at her side. They couldn't help. They were simply waiting for the one update they yearned for and dreaded: that she had finally passed. And that took a week. The first night, I wrote an email to my distribution list.

My mom went into a coma this afternoon. She looks totally peaceful, is in no pain, and is home in her own room, just what she wanted. She had a good morning. She talked to my brother, several relatives, and missed a few, too. She was on an energy surge. I have been told that is normal at the point before going into either a coma or death. I expect that she won't last too much longer.

She had a long time to say goodbye, reflect on her life and how many people care for her, etc. I cannot think of even one thing that would have made her passing any better for her.

The next day, my husband flew to Florida for the week to attend to his dad's funeral. He was shocked and sad about his dad and my mom, and was worried about his own mother's health, too. It felt surreal to us that his dad's wife had also died recently.

With both Kato and John now out of the picture, I was the sole caregiver for Mom. I quickly found out that caregiving for someone in a coma was still a lot of physical work, as well as emotionally draining. I launched into a new "coma" routine consisting of personal hygiene tasks, such as brushing Mom's teeth, flipping her over so she wouldn't develop sores, lubricating her skin, giving her drops of pain medications, and adjusting her oxygen. I gave her drops of water and put

Chapstick on her lips. She was still on the oxygen machine but was not getting any nourishment, in accordance with her wishes for only drops of morphine and water.

The first few days, I curled up with her on her bed and talked with her about her life, my family's life, and whatever I could think of. I thought talking to her, keeping her mind alert, might somehow bring her back—even if just for a brief moment—to say goodbye. I hate to admit it; I still believed she might suddenly wake up. I read to her from an autobiography she had written about her life many years before. I talked about the photos, laughing and hoping that somewhere in her limp body, there was an inkling of what I had said. I played her favorite music for her, and put fresh flowers in her room.

During this time, a few close friends and a cousin told me that they believed a person in a coma was aware of what was happening around them. They thought that my mom could hear what I was saying. I wasn't sure about that, but just in case, I kept talking to her. I gave her updates on John's Florida trip, recapped email messages that I had received from relatives, and was in and out of her room constantly during the day.

I tried to sleep in my own bed the following nights, but on night two of the coma, I ended up sleeping on the floor in Mom's room. I wasn't really getting much sleep anyway. I knew she was going to pass, and felt I should be there.

The kids had to keep up their routine, so a dear friend (thank you Pam) picked them up and dropped them back home from high school each day. They were uncharacteristically quiet during those days—very somber and sad. It must have been difficult for them to leave the house, not knowing if their Granny might be dead upon their return.

I wasn't overly supportive of them at the time. I feel bad about that, especially given their dad was in Florida and they had lost their grandfather too, but I was singularly focused on Mom. None of us can remember if we talked about the situation, or what our family evenings were like during those days. They were in the midst of finals that week, and I don't even remember bugging them to study.

One of my closest friends brought the kids a pizza dinner that first night, and sat with me for a time (thank you for your loving friendship, Terry). We watched Mom's every breath. Every minute felt like an eternity. Her breathing pattern would change slightly, and I'd lean forward, holding her hand, waiting for the last breath to come. It seemed like such a frail little thing couldn't last for long. Terry finally needed to go, as she was leaving the next day for a lengthy trip. I was sad she couldn't be with me those final days.

My husband kept in touch but was getting his dad's things in order, arranging the funeral and such. Over the following days, friends were also in touch—Terry's husband Dave (love you and miss you, my rock) was one of them—and they offered all kinds of support and expressions of love. Yet, I still felt quite alone, with nothing to distract me from the waiting. It was agony.

Diane's journal: Can a person choose when to let go?

Being alone was probably one reason I journaled and wrote emails to my relatives. Writing to them gave me a sense of connection. Or maybe it was a way to release my emotional energy each night. Perhaps it was both of those things.

The next few days were a blur, but here are a few of the emails.

Well, thought I'd give you my update for the day. Her nurse just left, and my mom is hanging in there for now. The nurse said it could be anytime, or as much as a few days. It is hard to believe that someone so tiny and frail can still be alive. The nurse gave me some signs to look for to identify when things are running down. My mom does not appear to be in any pain or discomfort, and in fact, looks like a little angel, all wrapped up in her blankets.

I have my mom's favorite CD on. I don't think she can really hear it, probably, but figured it wouldn't hurt to play it in the background. We have cats, which aren't allowed in her room, but I had let them in to lay next to me last night when I was sitting with my mom. The nurse said that when I was telling her (the nurse) that I had let the cats in, that my mom's breathing rate increased, so maybe she is still aware at some level, and guess I need to keep those demon cats out of there. I still talk to her just in case. I keep asking her where her angels are. I'm sure they will be coming soon.

But the angels didn't come. Each day, I dreaded checking her, thinking she had passed. Each day, our boys went to school not knowing what would await them upon their return. I was sleep-deprived and getting confused. John tried to keep in touch but was busy. He reached out to other friends to be sure people were connecting with me each day. Friends called and suggested that perhaps my mom was waiting for John's return before she passed, so I'd have his support. Given he wasn't due home for several days, this was not a pleasant thought.

She wasn't receiving any nourishment other than drops of water. She was literally wasting away before my eyes. Her lips were very chapped, and her skin was papery and dry. I tried to put cream and Chapstick on her, but nothing seemed to help. I needed her to let go and told her that she could, even with John absent. The next email talked about this.

People keep telling me maybe she is waiting for John to return from Florida, which will probably be Friday. That is a frightening thought for me; I am emotionally and physically exhausted at this point.

I told her this morning that I need her to pass. Where are those angels?

But she wasn't ready to go. The next day was my father-in-law's funeral. My email update that day read:

That night, I told Mom I was going to sleep in my own bed and not on her floor. I needed sleep. I kissed her and told her I loved her. I also told her goodbye and went upstairs to bed. That next morning, I avoided rushing downstairs, but eventually found my way down to her room. She was still breathing—both a shock and a source of contentment for me. Hard to explain. I didn't want to lose her, but I didn't want her to live like that, and knew it was simply a matter of time. How could such a frail little ninety-three-year-old woman continue to hang on? Especially when I knew she was ready to go.

I don't recall exactly what I did each day. Most of the time, I was in Mom's room, talking with her, caring for her, and writing in my journal.

The next day was our sons' last day of school, and John was coming home. I thought if Mom was waiting for his return, thank goodness he'd be home soon. Before I went to bed that night, I sent out a short email.

168

I don't know why she is hanging on. The weather here has been overcast and gloomy — maybe she is waiting for a beam of sunlight to show her the way?

John had experienced an emotional, gut-wrenching week; planning his dad's funeral, and then sorting through his dad's lifetime accumulation of "stuff," selling a car, and dealing with other family matters. The family was still suffering from the loss of his stepmom a few months earlier. So much trauma.

The next morning, I tiptoed downstairs to find Mom still breathing. I sat with her and once again pleaded with her to let go. She was suffering from dehydration; every wrinkle was becoming greatly pronounced. Her skin was dry, and her lips were cracked. I made deals with her. *I will do this if you pass. I will do that if you pass. The angels are waiting.* But she hung on. I made deals with God as well. I wasn't sure if He was listening, but figured it couldn't hurt.

My husband finally returned, and before he even sat down, I made him go into her room and talk to her. I made him tell her that he was home and that she could leave now, that he'd help take care of things, that he was there for me.

I wrote an email that afternoon.

My mom is still holding on. The nurse said today that all of the hospice people were totally amazed. That is my mom for you. Amazing and inspiring.

She seems determined to stay, for some unknown reason. I asked my husband to say, "I'm home now, goodbye," to her early this

*morning, in case that was why she was waiting, but she is still
here. Today is my cousin Cornelia's birthday, and I was
thinking, "She won't pass on Cornelia's birthday," so another
day perhaps.*

*I will keep you all posted. I hold her hand and play music for
her. I think she likes all the attention.*

The kids said another goodbye that night. They were relieved to be out of school, and happy their dad was back.

I went to check on her for the night, and something didn't seem normal in her breathing, so I sat down and hung around. John came in and stayed with me. I told him I thought she was finally letting go. A half hour or so later, her breathing became erratic. I held her hand, and she took one final deep breath and quietly passed. I was so glad John was with me and that we were there with her. Maybe she *had* hung on until his return.

I knew it was coming, but still, I was so upset. I held her hands tightly. I was surprised at how quickly her body became pale, cold, and stiff. My husband called the hospice nurse, who called the funeral home people, and they came to take her away. That, too, was very hard. I heard the zip of whatever they were taking her in, and then she was gone. Her comfy red flannel PJs and snuggly fuzzy socks were folded up on her bed. I've never been able to get rid of them.

I sent an email saying Mom finally got her wings. I'm sure it was a huge relief to all on the distribution list.

Even though I knew it was coming, I collapsed in exhaustion and grief.

Chapter 16

When your loved one passes

It was difficult telling our sons that their little Granny had died. Even though they knew it was coming, I'm not sure they believed it was really going to happen. I know they weren't sure what to say or do. Everyone walked around on eggshells for several days.

Relatives sent notes of sympathy and love. I'm sure they were relieved. My emails wore on them; it was a slow end. Friends and neighbors started hearing the news, and many reached out to me to express their sympathies. Talking to people was emotionally exhausting.

I cried a lot. For the first day or so, I sat in my mom's room for hours at a time. But I knew I needed to snap out of it and get to work on the funeral planning.

I spent days creating her obituary, and weeks working on a program for her and John's dad's memorial service. Even though my father-in-law, Joe, had a funeral in Florida, we decided to include a celebration of his life along with Mom's. That way, the kids and I could honor him along with saying goodbye to Granny.

My dad, my father-in-law Joe, and Mom on our wedding day

Truth #18: Funerals can be a wonderful distraction

Planning the funeral kept me from focusing on missing my mom. Going to the mortuary, I had to laugh, as the frugality that I inherited from my parents was put to the test. Would I be interested in a chipped urn that was at a greatly reduced price? Yes, I would. Did I want to pay for the upgrade to have music in the limo that carried the urn to the cemetery? No, I wouldn't.

I mean, who was going to hear it? The driver? I left with a free calendar and mortuary-logoed garment bag.

The funeral was lovely, and there was a good turnout. Mom used to say that everyone she knew would be dead by the time she passed away. Most of the people who came were our friends and neighbors, not my mom's and dad's peers. But the Lunch Bunch was there in full attendance, along with Jane, a lifelong friend of Mom's. My brother and his daughters flew out from the East Coast. My parents' nieces, Cornelia and Susan, were also there, my in-laws as well.

Cornelia wrote a beautiful tribute to my mom and dad. It was all about their kindness and focus on family. I was moved by her story of how my parents had positively influenced her life. Susan read a lovely passage my mom had chosen. A neighbor (thank you, dear Ginny) sang the songs my mom had picked out. They were beautiful, and I think Mom might have been brought to tears if she could have heard Ginny's lovely voice.

I made a "memory room" out of Mom's bedroom, half with things celebrating her life (photos, collectibles, quilts, and crafts) and half celebrating John's dad (with photos and a wide assortment of memorabilia from his time in the service).

I spent a lot of time attempting to write the perfect obit for Mom. How do you summarize a life in 500 words or less? I definitely tried. Along with all the usual obit facts and dates, I wrote, *"She was a real Southern lady with a sweet Southern accent and a tiny stature—people always said she was the 'cutest' thing. Her sweet nature somewhat hid her feistiness. She was incredibly open-minded and quite liberal in her views, had a keen sense of humor, and would always (politely) state her mind on any social or political issue. Her mind was sharp until the end. She was a kind and selfless person, and she inspired most everyone who knew her."*

In looking back, I don't think the obit truly captured what a strong woman she was all her life. But as she stated many years earlier, when a relative had died and she was reading his obit, "500 words isn't enough to capture the magnitude of one's accomplishments throughout a life." She was a gifted writer herself; I wish I had thought to have her write her own obituary.

A few of my friends set up a beautiful buffet at the funeral. Many people brought dishes or sent gorgeous flower bouquets. It was lovely; the weather was perfect, and we could spend time sitting outside in the garden that she loved.

I so appreciated everyone who attended. I don't know if people realize how special it is, when someone elderly dies, for anyone, no matter how well they knew them, to pay their respects. It was very meaningful to our entire family to have friends and neighbors come by.

When the funeral was over, I finally stopped "doing things" and breathed. I checked in on our sons, and took a moment. I slept for nearly fourteen hours that night. Then it was time to get moving again.

Truth #19: No-one wants most of the "precious" stuff

After the funeral, I continued to focus on the aftermath of Mom's death, packing up her room, keeping busy with estate activities, and doing anything to fill the caregiving void. Plus, there were a lot of things that needed doing. But suddenly, I had a lot of time in my day. It felt uncomfortable. It made me anxious. Walking by her room was tough.

As I went through her things, I realized that a lifetime of someone's precious stuff was not necessarily precious stuff. Oh, there were definitely a few special items I still have: her talking clock that sounds like a rooster, her wedding ring, and a few other personal items. But there were so many things that needed to go (though not without a little smile), including her twelve pairs of eyeglasses and her collection of rain bonnets. It was funny—an elderly woman, who never went out in the rain, owned fifteen of those little logoed plastic rain bonnets that companies used to give away.

She loved roses and did paint-by-numbers and stitchery of roses. On the backs of her works, she'd penciled in the names of those who should receive them. There were all her quilts (stored for our boys), some memorabilia, and many craft items—but frankly, other than photos, not a lot of treasures desirable to her grandkids. As I mentioned, today's kids don't seem to want their grandparents' antiques and fine china.

Pretty much everything we had stored for nine years in our storage unit was discarded.

I found several emotional treasures in her closet: an old suitcase containing many of the cards I had sent to her and my dad, letters she had sent to her mom early in her marriage, old documents, and some family photos. Many of these were things I had not previously seen.

After a few months of accounting, packing, discarding, and organizing, my job as a caregiver (and executor of my parents' trust) was done. I was no longer a caregiver or a daughter. Now what was I supposed to do?

Chapter 17

Surviving loss and grieving one's caregiving role

Don't cry because it's over. Smile because it happened.
Theodor Geisel, Dr. Seuss

After the funeral and cleaning through my mom's things, I experienced bouts of anxiety and depression. Sure, I missed Mom, but it was much more than that. I felt dangerously sad and nervous all the time.

Months went by. I didn't know what was going on, but at the same time, our older son was beginning to apply for college, and the other one wasn't too far behind him. We also started talking about selling our sweet little cabin since we weren't using it much and were facing two sets of college expenses. I attributed my sadness to still missing Mom, and my anxiety to an impending empty nest and lots of future changes.

But the feelings didn't improve. My husband tried to do what he could to distract me and cheer me up, but it was difficult for him, given that I couldn't really explain why I felt so sad and lost. Even months later, I felt uneasy, as if I should be doing something I wasn't doing. Time continued to crawl. As a caregiver, my schedule was structured and busy, but now the days dragged on and on. I tried to occupy myself with volunteer work. I became hyper-focused on my two sons and their variety of to-dos relating to school, college prep, and Scouts.

I was grieving, but not simply grieving the loss of my mother. I was grieving the loss of my longtime identity and purpose. I spent so much of each day as a caregiver for over a decade, and in her final months, Mom was like a newborn infant needing constant care. Then suddenly, all of that was gone. And she was gone, too.

Even more time passed. I was functioning, but trying to hide how I felt from my family and friends. Eventually, I couldn't hide it any longer. I was really struggling. It was an "unable to do" moment for me. I finally went to see a therapist.

The therapist (thanks, Carolyn) suggested both therapy and anxiety medication. She talked a lot about the "transition" that I was in: how caregivers leave their previous life and identity behind, in a way, and then are so busy caregiving—especially at the end of their loved one's journey—that they often aren't prepared for the transition back to who they previously were. After their loved one dies, they realize that they haven't had the time, energy, or psychological will to lay the groundwork for what comes next.

I saw this with Mom when my father had died. The pattern of her daily life was completely defined by her caregiving role, and when Dad died, it took her a while to adjust to a new routine and a new identity. She was also no longer part of a couple, which I think was quite difficult for her. Being a widow completely altered her future path. And like me, she hadn't had time to think about it—or mentally prepare for it—prior to the transition happening.

While I was initially resistant to the idea of anxiety medication, I feel it helped "lift the dark cloud" hanging over me. After starting it, one day, I woke up and felt immensely better. It wasn't long before I felt well enough to stop taking it.

The therapy also helped me understand how my perfectionist personality was at odds with the reality of caring for someone who was dying. It helped me accept that no matter how perfect of a caregiver I tried to be, that I was not superhuman, and didn't have superpowers. It helped me accept that I did my best to help Mom live a happy life and remain at home with her family. I needed to stop feeling guilty and focus on all the good that I did. Instead of remembering moments of impatience, I needed to reflect on all the moments of love and kindness we had shared together. I don't know why "former" caregivers are so focused on their (usually minor) failings, but in most of the people I interviewed, that seemed to be the case. *What didn't they do well?*

As I look back, how a caregiver feels after their loved one dies makes so much sense. My mental state was simply an inability to let go—not only of my mom, but the responsibility, focus, and intensity of caregiving itself. I truly believe the loss of the caregiving role was the basis of so much of the emptiness I was feeling at the time. Of course I missed Mom, but I was relieved when she died because she was no longer in pain. She was ready to go. But I missed the role of being her lifeline.

Remember early in this book when I created a "new normal" when Mom moved in with my family? Well, it was time to do that again—to create a new normal from what I had been focused on for the last decade. I needed to go back to being a full-time wife and mother. I had to create new routines, reclaim old interests, and redefine my identity. With a son heading out to college and the process of selling our cabin starting, I had a lot of distractions around that time, which was probably a good thing. Once we navigated some of those changes, I seemed to pop back to the surface and got back into freelancing. I found myself again. I had new priorities and a renewed sense of purpose. The grief lessened. I finally made it to the other side of the mountain.

Truth #20: Show the love while your loved ones are alive

I think about my parents often, and feel that my mom is somehow still with me. When I see some of her things in our new house, or when I am in the garden, I can still feel her nearby. I'm glad I summoned her spirit to move with us. I believe that, in some manner, she did make the trip to our new home and is with us today.

I know both of my parents knew I loved them. I expressed it in every card I sent them throughout their lives. Within each Hallmark greeting, there was always a handwritten, personalized note expressing some uniqueness about them, some quality that was special. I also showed them my love through my actions and by involving them in my family's life. But I have to admit that I did not always *tell* them I loved them outside of greeting cards, health emergencies or hospital settings. Sometimes *saying* "I love you," and holding a parent's hands on a normal day, simply doesn't happen. I'm so happy when my sons say to my husband or me, "I love you," for no particular reason. It is so powerful.

And while we may tell our family and loved ones that we love them, we often don't express *why* we love them—and that's important, too. It's more personal and precise. Sure, we write wonderful obits after our loved one has passed, but those are usually more fact-based, and often don't capture how truly wonderful they were, or what an effect they had on us. Plus, they aren't around to hear it anyway; it's too late.

How many of us don't tell our loved ones how we feel until we are standing at their gravesite? I know that I shared many personal and emotional thoughts about my dad at his funeral, that I likely never told him directly. I shared special memories that were all about what an influence he had on my life. I wish I had been able to share them with him before he had passed, and not just in front of his urn. During my interviews, I heard many caregivers express regret for not telling their loved one how special they were to them, and why.

Not long after Mom moved in with my family, I thought about this. What prompted me was the death of someone in our extended family. I mentioned this earlier, that my mother had felt that the obituary didn't truly honor the person or capture all they had been. In her view, the obit hadn't told why the individual was so loved and special.

That night, I jotted down a letter to Mom in my journal titled, "The Wonder of Granny," and then read it to her the next day. She was very touched, and even suggested that I try to publish it. I submitted it to a local newspaper featuring a section focused on personal stories. And guess what? It was published. One of my first published pieces, I still have the clippings.

I encourage everyone to share their love, admiration, and respect while their loved one is still alive and able to relish the words. Saying, "I love you," on a normal day, can be quite meaningful.

Diane's journal: The Wonder of Granny

We take so much for granted in life—our parents' love, for one thing.

As a parent now myself, I realize the daily sacrifices you and Dad made in raising your two children. You raised us to be good people. You showed us by example to be hard working, to pinch pennies, and to value friendships. You showed us by example to respect one's spouse, to respect the law, and to be proud of our country. Morality, ethics, religion… you and Dad charted a path for us. We didn't always take the path, but inevitably, we came back to it before straying once more.

I grew up feeling loved and cherished. And although I was adopted, it has absolutely never mattered to me. The daily caring and all the things that parents do over the course of a child's life made you my mom more than any biological connection could ever do.

As I got older and went to college, you were always there for me. I'd get a letter once a week with encouragement and a few bucks, which were both very needed. I may have seemed totally independent, but the emotional umbilical cord was still there. And you were still nourishing me through it.

You had a way of talking to me without talking down to me. When I was having a problem, you represented it as something that needed fixing, not that I needed fixing. There is a difference, and it made a difference in your realizing that.

Before you moved in with my family, my kids hardly knew you. They thought of you as fragile and serious. Their relationship with you now is so very different. They still see you as fragile, but they now see you as a special friend. They think about you even before I do— "What about Granny?" they'll say to me if we're going someplace or doing something. Someone they can go hang out with, someone that will tease them or that they can play a joke on, and someone (else) they can try and manipulate into giving them popcorn. I think it will be incredibly hard for them the day you are no longer with us. They love you so much.

Having you live with us has been a blessing. Oh, sometimes I do yearn to be alone at the house, to crank up my music or something. But these moments are few. More often, I use you to blow off steam or to chat with you about that day's top news horror or neighborhood gossip. I enjoy your sense of humor when you partner with John to tease the kids or me. I appreciate you biting your lip and not complaining when the dinner is burnt or when some other crisis occurs during our busy day. Sometimes I try to put myself in your place, and wonder what you think about our life… so hectic, sometimes so stressful. But we are a family, and life goes on.

And time passes. I wish I had more time, all of the time. But that's something I can't control. If there was more time, I would like to do things with you just for our enjoyment. You'd love the beauty of Bonfante Gardens, or going to an opera. There are so many things that you would enjoy, should enjoy. But there isn't enough time, with the kids and the house, and the obligations.

So, the time we spend together isn't always quality. It often is just time spent together, sharing a busy day.

Know, too, that I love you. Over the past few years, there have been several times when you were on death's door, in the hospital, about to have dangerous surgery and the like. Each of these times, I have held your hand and said "I love you" so many times. Yet, on any given day, I rarely say these words to you. They somehow seem out of place during a normal day when crisis isn't at hand. I don't know why.

But let me say it now, again.

I love you. I appreciate you. Thank you.

Chapter 18

Epilogue

For Mom's funeral, I wrote a tribute for my husband to read. I talked about many aspects of what made my mom unique, especially her kindness and focus on others. She was a wonderful and inspirational caregiver for my dad. She always surrounded herself with family and communities of interest, and put a lot of energy into those around her. She was not really a social butterfly, but she cherished—and nourished—her friendships deeply.

Her penmanship was exquisite, and until her eyesight deteriorated, she wrote these amazingly beautiful letters—lovely in both content and gorgeous cursive. She always sent Christmas cards—a habit passed on to me that I still prioritize today.

When she could no longer see well, and her writing got wobbly, she switched to the phone, and it became her lifeline. She made a point of calling people she thought she could cheer up. She even kept a current list of four or five people she should call, simply to say hello. This list was not necessarily the people she wanted to talk with the most. It was often people she felt would be happiest to hear from her.

I benefited a lot from having her as my mom, but perhaps even more from having the honor of being her caregiver. Many caregiver blessings will be with me throughout the remainder of my life, and every caregiver I interviewed expressed similar feelings. No matter what stresses occurred during their caregiving journey, they still felt it was a positive, life-changing experience for them—and, in many cases, the same was true for their families, which they wouldn't have traded for anything.

While this book was intentionally focused more on the mental and emotional "stressings" side of my caregiving story, please know that I could write volumes sharing all of the wonderful and positive moments that came out of my family's caregiving journeys with both of my parents. I treasure all of those experiences. I feel so fortunate to have videos, in particular, from the years Mom lived with us (especially videos that include Mom and Gramma with our sons). I wish we'd owned a video-camera back when Dad was alive, although I do have a recording of our father-daughter dance at my wedding. Such special memories.

If you are a caregiver, remember: don't do it alone, and don't forget that you aren't superhuman. Practice self-care early and often; you're not being selfish. Cut yourself some slack, don't listen to that inner voice of guilt, and don't second-guess yourself with "what ifs." Have faith. Be present, join your care receiver's journey, and relish every moment with them. Don't forget to breathe, laugh, and sing along the way. Let go when you're able to, and celebrate what you accomplished.

My mom taught me so much over the years. Keep calm. Be flexible. Treat everyone fairly. Be kind. Express optimism (or at least a positive pessimism if you must). Surround yourself with loved ones. Quality with people is better than quantity of

186

things. Wear rose-colored glasses. Imperfect is okay as long as you try your best. Laugh. Take one day at a time, stay present in that day and with those around you. The best life happens when there is a village of care—that and a bit of good gossip. Leave the world a better place.

Thanks mom. *I love you and Dad.*

And thanks for passing along the caregiving gene.

In remembrance

Photo courtesy of Susan C. Bryan

This Year Without My Mom

This year, there has been no sweet southern lady in the downstairs room;
the tiny scraping of her walker… silenced now.
This year, I go shopping and reach for her favorite food;
and then I stop, and think. Oh, how I miss her.

It's been almost a year since my mom passed away.
A year of reflection and memories; most good, some bad.
I miss the chance to chat; she, a part of my life and routine.
The silence is quite loud. Her room now so still.

This year, winter came and went; oh, how she hated the cold;
the rainy days even drearier without her bundled up presence.
Now, warm days… finally. Cats stretched out in beams of sunlight.
She was like them, always able to find that single spot of warmth and light.

This year, spring now fully upon us; the roses in bloom; her favorite.
Beautiful funeral gifts, planted in desolate spots, spring forth with grace;
five shades of pink, purples and reds; fragrant and so lovely.
Every time I am in the garden, I am with her. Remembering…

Her politeness, the gratitude always expressed for her care;
the unconditional love; always an open heart.
The determination to not be a burden; but how could she have been!
Petite and frail, yet strong in so many ways.

This year, still sorting through her things; a composite of her life.
Not wanting to discard her favorite robe, silly I know.
I am surrounded by her roses: pictures of her cherished roses, everywhere.
Look closely and you might see an angel reflected in their blooms.

This year, looking through old photos. You see the sweetness in her face.
Wishing for one more goodbye. Simply one more exchange;
but this year, and forever, there can just be memories; most good, some bad.
And days in the garden; moments in the sun. To remember.

Bibliography

1. Muennig, P., Jiao, B., & Singer, E. (2018). Living with parents or grandparents increases social capital and survival: 2014 General Social Survey-National Death Index. *SSM - Population Health, 4,* 71-75. https://doi.org/10.1016/j.ssmph.2017.11.001

2. You W, Henneberg M. (2022). Large household reduces dementia mortality: A cross-sectional data analysis of 183 populations. *PLoS ONE* 17(3): e0263309.

3. Blazina, C. (2024, April 14). More than half of Americans in their 40s are 'sandwiched' between an aging parent and their own children. *Pew Research Center.* https://www.pewresearch.org/fact-tank/2022/04/08/more-than-half-of-americans-in-their-40s-are-sandwiched-between-an-aging-parent-and-their-own-children/

4. Weber-Raley, L., National Alliance for Caregiving, Caring Across Generations, & MassMutual's SpecialCare SM program. (2019). Burning the candle at both ends: Sandwich generation caregiving in the U.S, *NATIONAL REPORT.* https://caringacross.org/wp-content/uploads/2024/01/NAC_SandwichCaregiving_Report_digital112019.pdf

5. de Visé, D. (2023, November 17). What is the "sandwich generation"? Many adults struggle with caregiving, bills and work. *USA TODAY.* Retrieved September 12, 2024. https://www.usatoday.com/story/money/2023/11/17/sandwich-generation-helping-parents-children/71590330007/

6. Efron, S. (2019, March 1). An aging population creates a "Nursing hell" for many women. *Los Angeles Times.* Retrieved September 12, 2024. https://www.latimes.com/archives/la-xpm-2001-jun-25-mn-14481-story.

7. Mitchell, T., & Mitchell, T. (2024, April 14). Financial issues top the list of reasons U.S. adults live in multigenerational homes. *Pew Research Center.* https://www.pewresearch.org/social-trends/2022/03/24/financial-issues-top-the-list-of-reasons-u-s-adults-live-in-multigenerational-homes/

8. Span, P. (2017, July 3). Years later, divorce complicates caregiving. *The New Old Age Blog.* Retrieved September 12, 2024. https://archive.nytimes.com/newoldage.blogs.nytimes.com/2009/08/10/years-later-divorce-complicates-caregiving/

9. Accius, J., PhD. (2023, November 28). Breaking Stereotypes: Spotlight on male family caregivers. *AARP.* https://www.aarp.org/pri/topics/ltss/family-caregiving/breaking-stereotypes-spotlight-on-male-family-caregivers/

10. Smith KE, Porges EC, Norman GJ, et al. Oxytocin receptor gene variation predicts empathic concern and autonomic arousal while perceiving harm to others. *Soc Neurosci.* 2014 Feb;9(1):1-9.

11. Ansberry, C. (2023, October 24). More Men Are Taking Care of Aging Parents. They Feel Unprepared. *The Wallstreet Journal.* Retrieved September 11, 2024. https://www.wsj.com/health/wellness/men-caregivers-aging-parents-sons-ba7a6d71

12. *Caregiver statistics: Work and Caregiving - Family Caregiver Alliance.* (2022, December 2). Family Caregiver Alliance. Retrieved September 11, 2024. https://www.caregiver.org/resource/caregiver-statistics-work-and-caregiving/

13. Whiting, C. G., Reinhard, S., Heinz, P. A., et al. (2020) *Caregiving in the U.S. 2020 [Report]* https://www.caregiving.org/wp-content/uploads/2021/01/full-report-caregiving-in-the-united-states-01-21.pdf

14. Committee on Family Caregiving for Older Adults; Board on Health Care Services; Health and Medicine Division; National Academies of Sciences, Engineering, and Medicine; Schulz R, Eden J, editors. Families Caring for an Aging America. Washington (DC): National Academies Press (US); 2016 Nov 8. 3, Family Caregiving Roles and Impacts. https://www.ncbi.nlm.nih.gov/books/NBK396398/

15. Age Wave. (2019, February 7). *Age Wave*. Retrieved September 12, 2024. https://agewave.com/what-we-do/landmark-research-and-consulting/research-studies/leaving-a-legacy-a-lasting-gift-to-loved-ones/

16. Peacock, K., Carlson, K., & Ketvertis, K. M. (2023, December 21). *Menopause*. StatPearls - NCBI Bookshelf. https://www.ncbi.nlm.nih.gov/books/NBK507826

17. *Women and Caregiving: Facts and figures - Family Caregiver Alliance*. (2023, March 13). Family Caregiver Alliance. Retrieved September 12, 2024. https://www.caregiver.org/resource/women-and-caregiving-facts-and-figures/

18. Rollet, J. (2023, September 29). Menopause symptoms worsen with caregiver burden. *Healio*. Retrieved September 12, 2024. https://www.healio.com/news/womens-health-ob-gyn/20230929/menopause-symptoms-worsen-with-caregiver-burden

19. *80% of caregivers report strain on their marriages - Caring.com*. (2022, August 10). Caring.com. Retrieved September 12, 2024. https://www.caring.com/about/news-room/press-release-caregiver-marital-stress/

20. Donna Benton, Thomas Dudley, Marty Ford, et al. (2015). *Caregiving in the U.S. 2015 report*. https://www.aarp.org/content/dam/aarp/ppi/2015/caregiving-in-the-united-states-2015-report-revised.pdf

21. Accius, J., PhD. (2023, November 28). Breaking Stereotypes: Spotlight on male family caregivers. *AARP*. https://www.aarp.org/pri/topics/ltss/family-caregiving/breaking-stereotypes-spotlight-on-male-family-caregivers/

22. Yoshikawa Y, Ohmaki E, Kawahata H, et al. Beneficial effect of laughter therapy on physiological and psychological function in elders. *Nurs Open*. 2018 Jul 18;6(1):93-99.

23. Ruch, W., Platt, T., Proyer, R. T., et al. (2019). Editorial: Humor and Laughter, Playfulness and Cheerfulness: Upsides and downsides to a life of lightness. *Frontiers in Psychology, 10*. https://doi.org/10.3389/fpsyg.2019.00730

24. *The dangers of polypharmacy and the case for deprescribing in older adults*. (2021, August 24). National Institute on Aging. Retrieved September 12, 2024.https://www.nia.nih.gov/news/dangers-polypharmacy-and-case-deprescribing-older-adults

25. Hales CM, Servais J, Martin CB, et al. (2019) *Prescription drug use among adults aged 40–79 in the United States and Canada*. NCHS Data Brief, no 347. Hyattsville, MD: National Center for Health Statistics. https://www.cdc.gov/nchs/products/databriefs/db347.htm

26. FDA. (2021). *Watch Out for False Promises About So-Called Alzheimer's Cures*. US Food & Drug Administration. Retrieved September 12, 2024. https://www.fda.gov/consumers/consumer-updates/watch-out-false-promises-about-so-called-alzheimers-cures

Why I incorporated "other loved souls"

While neither of my parents experienced dementia, an increasing number of caregivers must manage through that additional challenge. I wanted to include their stories.

Consequently, I interviewed over a dozen caregivers—many having a loved one with Alzheimer's—to add their personal insights on caregiving. Much of what they had to say dealt with the mental and emotional stress surrounding the disease and its heartbreaking progression.

These interviews enabled me to incorporate stories from a wide variety of caregiving scenarios and cover a number of issues that I didn't personally face while caring for my own parents—including struggles with extended family, financial stress, etc. I was also able to include the unique perspectives of several male caregivers—all of whom definitely had "the gene."

The voices and narrative belonging to these "other loved souls" have been an ongoing source of inspiration to me while writing this book. I hope my including their thoughts will benefit you, the reader, as well.

Acknowledgments

Special thanks to my husband and sons for being such an important part of Granny's caregiving team. I am forever grateful to them, as well as our extended family and the many friends who were so caring and loving to Mom and me.

Chris and Casey, your Granny and Grampa (and Papa Joe, too) would be so proud of you. I love you and your dad more than I can put into simple words.

Hugs and appreciation to the caregivers who allowed me the privilege to tell parts of their stories. It isn't always easy to reflect on a loved one's final years; caregiving memories can be bittersweet. I was sad to learn that one of these heroic caregivers (thank you so much, Kathleen) is now herself in a memory facility, underscoring how precious our time with loved ones truly is.

Heartfelt appreciation to Mom's hospice caregiver, Kato. You made a difficult time so much easier and peaceful.

Thanks to Chris Blum for the book's beautiful cover design.

Much gratitude to Harry Bryan, Tina Chan, and Cathryn Rakich for their incredible editorial assistance and guidance. You helped make this a better book.

About the author

Diane Doran Blum is a freelance writer working primarily in the holistic healthcare space. She writes from her home office, often wearing a robe and slippers, and usually with a cat on her lap. She is married and has two adult sons, two cats, and 27 fruit trees (at last count). She maintains a personal blog at www.ObsoletedSoccerMom.com where she records her thoughts on life, motherhood, being adopted, and the trials of getting older.

Reach her at *DianeDoranBlum@ObsoletedSoccerMom.com*